Ironworkers Apprenticeship Aptitude Test Prep

Ironworkers Apprenticeship Aptitude Study Guide and Practice Test Questions

Complete
Test Preparation Inc.
www.test-preparation.ca

Copyright © 2021 by Complete Test Preparation Inc. ALL RIGHTS RESERVED.

No part of this book may be reproduced or transferred in any form or by any means, graphic, electronic, or mechanical, including photocopying, recording, web distribution, taping, or by any information storage retrieval system, without the written permission of the author.

Notice: Complete Test Preparation Inc. makes every reasonable effort to obtain from reliable sources accurate, complete, and timely information about the tests covered in this book. Nevertheless, changes can be made in the tests or the administration of the tests at any time and Complete Test Preparation Inc. makes no representation or warranty, either expressed or implied as to the accuracy, timeliness, or completeness of the information contained in this book. Complete Test Preparation Inc. make no representations or warranties of any kind, express or implied, about the completeness, accuracy, reliability, suitability or availability with respect to the information contained in this document for any purpose. Any reliance you place on such information is therefore strictly at your own risk.

The author(s) shall not be liable for any loss incurred as a consequence of the use and application, directly or indirectly, of any information presented in this work. Sold with the understanding, the author is not engaged in rendering professional services or advice. If advice or expert assistance is required, the services of a competent professional should be sought.

The company, product and service names used in this publication are for identification purposes only. All trademarks and registered trademarks are the property of their respective owners. Complete Test Preparation Inc. is not affiliate with any educational institution.

Complete Test Preparation Inc. is not affiliated with, or endorsed by any official testing organization. All organizational and test names are trademarks of their respective owners.

We strongly recommend that students check with exam providers for up-to-date information regarding test content.

This product is provided for skill practice only

ISBN-13: 978-1-77245-504-5

Version 9 Updated June 2025

About Complete Test Preparation Inc.

Why Us?
The Complete Test Preparation Team has been publishing high quality study materials since 2005, with a catalogue of over 145 titles, in English, French and Chinese, as well as ESL curriculum for all levels.

To keep up with the industry changes, we update everything all the time!

And the best part?
With every purchase, you're helping people all over the world improve themselves and their education. So thank you in advance for supporting this mission with us! Together, we are truly making a difference in the lives of those often forgotten by the system.

Charities that we support
https://www.test-preparation.ca/charities-and-non-profits/

You have definitely come to the right place.
If you want to spend your valuable study time where it will help you the most - we've got you covered today and tomorrow.

FEEDBACK

We welcome your feedback. Email us at feedback@test-preparation.ca with your comments and suggestions. We carefully review all suggestions and often incorporate reader suggestions into upcoming versions. As a Print on Demand Publisher, we update our products frequently.

https://www.facebook.com/CompleteTestPreparation/

https://www.youtube.com/user/MrTestPreparation

CONTENTS

8   **Getting Started**
      How this study guide is organized   9
      The Ironworkers Test Study Plan   9
      Making a Study Schedule   10

15   **Reading Comprehension**
      Self Assessment   18
      Answer Key   28
      Help with Reading   Comprehension   32
      Main Idea and Supporting Details   35
      Drawing Inferences and Conclusions   39
      Meaning From Context   42

46   **Mathematics &Problem Solving**
      Math Self-Assessment   50
      Answer Key   61
      Basic math Video Tutorials   67
      Fraction Tips, Tricks and Shortcuts   67
      Decimal Tips, Tricks and Shortcuts   73
      Converting Decimals to Fractions   73
      Percent Tips, Tricks and Shortcuts   74
      Exponents – a Quick Tutorial   76
      Problem Solving   82
      Types of Problems   84
      Algebraic Equations   94
      Ratios   95
      Pythagorean Geometry   103
      Quadrilaterals   106
      Metric Conversion - A Quick Tutorial   108

111   **Mechanical Comprehension**
      Self-Assessment   113
      Answer Key   121
      Overview of Simple Machines   124

129	**Practice Test Questions Set 1**	
	Answer Key	177
201	**Practice Test Questions Set 2**	
	Answer Key	247
269	**Supplemental Practice**	
270	**Conclusion**	

Getting Started

CONGRATULATIONS! By deciding to take the Ironworkers Aptitude Test, you have taken the first step toward a great future! Of course, there is no point in taking this important examination unless you intend to do your best to earn the highest grade you possibly can. That means getting yourself organized and discovering the best approaches, methods and strategies to master the material. Yes, that will require real effort and dedication on your part, but if you are willing to focus your energy and devote the study time necessary, before you know it you will be on you way to a brighter future.

We know that taking on a new endeavour can be scary, and it is easy to feel unsure of where to begin. That's where we come in. This study guide is designed to help you improve your test-taking skills, show you a few tricks of the trade and increase both your competency and confidence.

The Ironworkers Aptitude Exam

The Ironworkers exam has three modules, basic math, problem solving (word problems) and reading comprehension.

While we seek to make our guide as comprehensive as possible, note that like all entrance exams, the Ironworkers Exam might be adjusted at some future point. New material might be added, or content that is no longer relevant or applicable might be removed. It is always a good idea to give the materials you receive when you register to take the Ironworkers test a careful review.

Getting Started

How this study guide is organized

This study guide is divided into three sections. The first section, Self-Assessments, which will help you recognize your areas of strength and weaknesses. This will be a boon when it comes to managing your study time most efficiently; there is not much point of focusing on material you have already got firmly under control. Instead, taking the self-assessments will show you where that time could be much better spent. In this area you will begin with a few questions to evaluate quickly your understanding of material that is likely to appear on the Ironworkers test. If you do poorly in certain areas, simply work carefully through those sections in the tutorials and then try the self-assessment again.

The second section, Tutorials, offers information in each of the content areas, as well as strategies to help you master that material. The tutorials are not intended to be a complete course, but cover general principles. If you find that you do not understand the tutorials, it is recommended that you seek out additional instruction.

Third, we offer two sets of practice test questions, similar to those on the Ironworkers exam. Again, we cover all modules, so make sure to check with your school!

The Ironworkers Test Study Plan

Now that you have made the decision to take the Ironworkers test, it is time to get started. Before you do another thing, you will need to figure out a plan of attack. The best study tip is to start early! The longer the time period you devote to regular study practice, the likelier that you will retain the material and access it quickly. If you thought that 1 x 20 is the same as 2 x 10, guess what? It really is not, when it comes to study time. Reviewing material for just an hour per day over the course of 20 days is far better than studying for two hours a day for only 10 days. The more often you revisit a particular piece of information, the better you will know it. Not only will your grasp and understanding be better, but your ability to reach into your brain and quickly and efficiently pull out the tidbit you need, will be greatly enhanced as well.

The great Chinese scholar and philosopher Confucius believed that true knowledge could be defined as knowing what you know and what you do not know. The first step in preparing for the Ironworkers test Exam is to assess your strengths and weaknesses. You may already have an idea of what you know and what you do not know, but evaluating yourself using our Self- Assessment modules for each of the three areas, Math, Problem Solving and Reading Comprehension, will clarify the details.

Making a Study Schedule

To make your study time the most productive, you will need to develop a study plan. The purpose of the plan is to organize all the bits of pieces of information in such a way that you will not feel overwhelmed. Rome was not built in a day, and learning everything you will need to know to pass the Ironworkers test is going to take time, too. Arranging the material you need to learn into manageable chunks is the best way to go. Each study session should make you feel as though you have accomplished your goal, or at least are a little closer, and your goal is simply to learn what you planned to learn during that particular session. Try to organize the content in such a way that each study session builds on previous ones. That way, you will retain the information, be better able to access it, and review the previous bits and pieces at the same time.

The Best Study Tip! The best study tip is to start early! The longer you study regularly, the more you will retain and 'learn' the material. Studying for 1 hour per day for 20 days is far better than studying for 2 hours for 10 days.

What don't you know?

The first step is to assess your strengths and weaknesses. You may already have an idea of where your weaknesses are, or you can take our Self-assessment modules for each of the areas, Math, English, Science and Reading Comprehension.

Exam Component	Rate from 1 to 5
Reading Comprehension	
Inferences and Conclusions	
Finding information in a passage	
Main Idea	
Basic Math	
Geometry	
Fractions Decimals Percent	
Algebra	
Exponents	
Metric Conversion	
Problem Solving	

Making a Study Schedule

The key to a successful study plan is to divide the material you need to learn into manageable size and learn it, while at the same time reviewing the material that you already know.

Using the table above, any scores of three or below, mean you need to spend time learning, reviewing and practicing this subject area. A score of four means you need to review the material, but you don't have to spend time re-learning. A score of five and you are OK with just an occasional review before the exam.

A score of zero or one means you really do need to work on this and you should allocate the most time and give it the highest priority. Some students prefer a 5-day plan and others a 10-day plan. It also depends on how much time you have until the exam.

Here is an example of a 5-day plan based on an example from the table above:

Reading Comprehension: 1   Study 1 hour everyday – review on last day
Fractions: 3   Study 1 hour for 2 days then ½ hour and then review
Algebra: 4   Review every second day
Exponents: 2 Study 1 hour on the first day – then ½ hour everyday
Reading Comprehension: 5   Review for ½ hour every other day
Geometry: 5 Review for ½ hour every other day

Using this example, geometry and reading comprehension are good and only need occasional review. Algebra is good and needs 'some' review. Fractions need a bit of work, grammar and usage needs a lot of work and Reading Comprehension is very weak and need most time. Based on this, here is a sample study plan:

Day	Subject	Time
Monday		
Study	Reading Comprehension	1 hour
Study	Exponents	1 hour
	½ hour break	
Study	Fractions	1 hour
Review	Algebra	½ hour
Tuesday		
Study	Reading Comprehension	1 hour
Study	Exponents	½ hour
	½ hour break	
Study	Fractions	½ hour
Review	Algebra	½ hour

Review	Geometry	½ hour
Wednesday		
Study	Reading Comprehension	1 hour
Study	Exponents	½ hour
	½ hour break	
Study	Fractions	½ hour
Review	Geometry	½ hour
Thursday		
Study	Reading Comprehension	½ hour
Study	Exponents	½ hour
Review	Fractions	½ hour
	½ hour break	
Review	Geometry	½ hour
Review	Algebra	½ hour
Friday		
Review	Reading Comprehension	½ hour
Review	Exponents	½ hour
Review	Fractions	½ hour
	½ hour break	
Review	Algebra	½ hour
Review	Exponents	½ hour

Using this example, adapt the study plan to your own schedule. This schedule assumes 2 ½ - 3 hours available to study everyday for a 5 day period.

First, write out what you need to study and how much. Next figure out how many days you have before the test. Note, do NOT study on the last day before the test. On the last day before the test, you won't learn anything and will probably only confuse yourself.

Make a table with the days before the test and the number of hours you have available to study each day. We suggest working with 1 hour and ½ hour time slots.

Start filling in the blanks, with the subjects you need to study the most getting the most time and the most regular time slots (i.e. everyday) and the subjects that you know getting the least time (e.g. ½ hour every other day, or every 3rd day).

Tips for making a schedule

Once you make a schedule, stick with it! Make your study sessions reasonable. If you make a study schedule and don't stick with it, you set yourself up for failure. Instead, schedule study sessions that are a bit shorter and set yourself up for success! Make sure your study sessions are do-able. Studying is hard work but after you pass, you can party and take a break!

Schedule breaks. Breaks are just as important as study time. Work out a rotation of studying and breaks that works for you.

Build up study time. If you find it hard to sit still and study for 1 hour straight through, build up to it. Start with 20 minutes, and then take a break. Once you get used to 20-minute study sessions, increase the time to 30 minutes. Gradually work you way up to 1 hour.

40 minutes to 1 hour is optimal. Studying for longer than this is tiring and not productive. Studying for shorter isn't long enough to be productive.

Studying Math. Studying Math is different from studying other subjects because you use a different part of your brain. The best way to study math is to practice everyday. This will train your mind to think in a mathematical way. If you miss a day or days, the mathematical mind-set is gone and you have to start all over again to build it up.

Study and practice math everyday for at least 5 days before the exam.

Reading Comprehension

THIS SECTION CONTAINS A SELF-ASSESSMENT AND READING TUTORIAL. The Tutorials are designed to familiarize general principles and the self-assessment contains general questions similar to the reading questions likely to be on the Ironworkers test exam, but are not intended to be identical to the exam questions. The tutorials are not designed to be a complete reading course, and it is assumed that students have some familiarity with reading comprehension questions. If you do not understand parts of the tutorial, or find the tutorial difficult, it is recommended that you seek out additional instruction.

Note that these questions are for skill practice only.

Tour of the Reading Content

The Ironworkers test reading section has 54 reading questions which includes reading comprehension and vocabulary. Below is a more detailed list of the types of reading questions that generally appear on the Ironworkers test.

- Drawing logical conclusions

- Identify the author's intent to persuade, inform, or entertain.

- Give the definition of a word from context

- Find specific information from a different types of communication (memo, posted notice etc.)

The questions below are not the same as you will find on the Ironworkers test - that would be too easy! And nobody knows what the questions will be and they change all the time. Mostly the changes consist of substituting new questions for old, but the changes can be new question formats or styles, changes to the number of questions in each section, changes to the time limits for each section and combining sections. Below are general reading questions that cover the same areas as the Ironworkers test. So, while the format and exact wording of the questions may differ slightly, and change from year to year, if you can answer the questions below, you will have no problem with the reading section of the Ironworkers test.

Reading Self-Assessment

The purpose of the self-assessment is:

- Identify your strengths and weaknesses.

- Develop your personalized study plan (above)

- Get accustomed to the Ironworkers test format

- Extra practice – the self-assessments are almost a full 3rd practice test!

- Provide a baseline score for preparing your study schedule.

Since this is a Self-assessment, and depending on how confident you are with Reading Comprehension, timing is optional.

Once complete, use the table below to assess your understanding of the content, and prepare your study schedule described in chapter 1.

80% - 100%	Excellent – you have mastered the content
60 – 79%	Good. You have a working knowledge. Even though you can just pass this section, you may want to review the Tutorials and do some extra practice to see if you can improve your mark.
40% - 59%	Below Average. You do not understand the reading comprehension problems. Review the tutorials, and retake this quiz again in a few days, before proceeding to the rest of the Practice Test Questions.
Less than 40%	Poor. You have a very limited understanding of the reading comprehension problems. Please review the Tutorials, and retake this quiz again in a few days, before proceeding to the Practice Test Questions.

READING COMPREHENSION SELF-ASSESSMENT

	A	B	C	D
1	○	○	○	○
2	○	○	○	○
3	○	○	○	○
4	○	○	○	○
5	○	○	○	○
6	○	○	○	○
7	○	○	○	○
8	○	○	○	○
9	○	○	○	○
10	○	○	○	○
11	○	○	○	○
12	○	○	○	○
13	○	○	○	○
14	○	○	○	○
15	○	○	○	○
16	○	○	○	○

Reading Comprehension

Directions: The following questions are based on several reading passages. A series of questions follow each passage. Read each passage carefully, and then answer the questions based on it. You may reread the passage as often as you wish. When you have finished answering the questions based on one passage, go right onto the next passage. Choose the best answer based on the information given and implied.

Questions 1 – 4 refer to the following passage.

Passage 1 - Who Was Anne Frank?

You may have heard mention of the word Holocaust in your History or English classes. The Holocaust took place from 1939-1945. It was an attempt by the Nazi party to purify the human race, by eliminating Jews, Gypsies, Catholics, homosexuals and others they deemed inferior to their "perfect" Aryan race. The Nazis used Concentration Camps, which were sometimes used as Death Camps, to exterminate the people they held in the camps. The saddest fact about the Holocaust was the over one million children under the age of sixteen died in a Nazi concentration camp. Just a few weeks before World War II was over, Anne Frank was one of those children to die.

Before the Nazi party began its persecution of the Jews, Anne Frank had a happy live. She was born in June of 1929. In June of 1942, for her 13th birthday, she was given a simple present which would go onto impact the lives of millions of people around the world. That gift was a small red diary that she called Kitty. This diary was to become Anne's most treasured possession when she and her family hid from the Nazi's in a secret annex above her father's office building in Amsterdam.

For 25 months, Anne, her sister Margot, her parents, another family, and an elderly Jewish dentist hid from the Nazis in this tiny annex. They were never permitted to go outside, and their food and supplies were brought to them by Miep Gies and her husband, who did not believe in the Nazi persecution of the Jews. It was a very difficult life for young Anne and she used Kitty as an outlet to describe her life in hiding.
After 2 years, Anne and her family were betrayed and ar-

rested by the Nazis. To this day, nobody is exactly sure who betrayed the Frank family and the other annex residents. Anne, her mother, and her sister were separated from Otto Frank, Anne's father. Then, Anne and Margot were separated from their mother. In March of 1945, Margot Frank died of starvation in a Concentration Camp. A few days later, at the age of 15, Anne Frank died of typhus. Of all the people who hid in the Annex, only Otto Frank survived the Holocaust.

Otto Frank returned to the Annex after World War II. It was there that he found Kitty, filled with Anne's thoughts and feelings about being a persecuted Jewish girl. Otto Frank had Anne's diary published in 1947 and it has remained continuously in print ever since. Today, the diary has been published in over 55 languages and more than 24 million copies have been sold around the world. The Diary of Anne Frank tells the story of a brave young woman who tried to see the good in all people.

1. From the context clues in the passage, what does annex mean?

    a. Attic

    b. Bedroom

    c. Basement

    d. Kitchen

Reading Comprehension

2. Why do you think Anne's diary has been published in 55 languages?

   a. So everyone could understand it.

   b. So people around the world could learn more about the horrors of the Holocaust.

   c. Because Anne was Jewish but hid in Amsterdam and died in Germany.

   d. Because Otto Frank spoke many languages.

3. From the description of Anne and Margot's deaths in the passage, what can we assume typhus is?

   a. The same as starving to death.

   b. An infection the Germans gave to Anne.

   c. A disease Anne caught in the concentration camp.

   d. Poison gas used by the Germans to kill Anne.

4. In the third paragraph, what does outlet mean?

   a. A place to plug things into the wall

   b. A store where Miep bought cheap supplies for the Frank family

   c. A hiding space similar to an Annex

   d. A place where Anne could express her private thoughts.

Questions 5 – 8 refer to the following passage.

Passage 2 - Was Dr. Seuss a Real Doctor?

A favorite author for over 100 years, Theodor Seuss Geisel was born on March 2, 1902. Today, we celebrate the birthday of the famous "Dr. Seuss" by hosting Read Across America events throughout the March. School children around the country celebrate the "Doctor's" birthday by making hats, giving presentations and holding read aloud circles featuring some of Dr. Seuss' most famous books.

But who was Dr. Seuss? Did he go to medical school? Where was his office? You may be surprised to know that Theodor Seuss Geisel was not a medical doctor at all. He took on the nickname Dr. Seuss when he became a noted children's book author. He earned the nickname because people said his books were "as good as medicine." All these years later, his nickname has lasted and he is known as Dr. Seuss all across the world.

Think back to when you were a young child. Did you ever want to try "green eggs and ham?" Did you try to "Hop on Pop?" Do you remember learning about the environment from a creature called The Lorax? Of course, you must recall one of Seuss' most famous characters; that green Grinch who stole Christmas. These stories were all written by Dr. Seuss and featured his signature rhyming words and letters. They also featured made up words to enhance his rhyme scheme and even though many of his characters were made up, they sure seem real to us today.

And what of his "signature" book, The Cat in the Hat? You must remember that cat and Thing One and Thing Two from your childhood. Did you know that in the early 1950's there was a growing concern in America that children were not becoming avid readers? This was, book publishers thought, because children found books dull and uninteresting. An intelligent publisher sent Dr. Seuss a book of words that he thought all children should learn as young readers. Dr. Seuss wrote his famous story The Cat in the Hat, using those words. We can see, over the decades, just how much influence his writing has had on very young children. That is why we celebrate this doctor's birthday each March.

5. What does the word "avid" mean in the last paragraph?

    a. Good

    b. Interested

    c. Slow

    d. Fast

6. What can we infer from the statement " His books were like medicine?"

    a. His books made people feel better

    b. His books were in doctor's office waiting rooms

    c. His books took away fevers

    d. His books left a funny taste in readers' mouths.

7. Why is the publisher in the last paragraph called "intelligent?"

    a. a. The publisher knew how to read.

    b. The publisher knew that kids did not like to read.

    c. The publisher knew Dr. Seuss would be able to create a book that sold well.

    d. The publisher knew that Dr. Seuss would be able to write a book that would get young children interested in reading.

8. The theme of this passage is

    a. Dr. Seuss was not a doctor.

    b. Dr. Seuss influenced the lives of generations of young children.

    c. Dr. Seuss wrote rhyming books.

    d. Dr. Seuss' birthday is a good day to read a book.

Questions 9 - 12 refer to the following passage.

Keeping Tropical Fish

Keeping tropical fish at home or in your office used to be very popular. Today, interest has declined, but it remains as rewarding and relaxing a hobby as ever. Ask any tropical fish hobbyist, and you will hear how soothing and relaxing watching colorful fish live their lives in the aquarium. If you are considering keeping tropical fish as pets, here is a list of the basic equipment you will need.

A filter is essential for keeping your aquarium clean and your fish alive and healthy. There are different types and sizes of filters and the right size for you depends on the size of the aquarium and the level of stocking. Generally, you need a filter with a 3 to 5 times turn over rate per hour. This means that the water in the tank should go through the filter about 3 to 5 times per hour.

Most tropical fish do well in water temperatures ranging between 24° C and 26° C, though each has its own ideal water temperature. A heater with a thermostat is necessary to regulate the water temperature. Some heaters are submersible and others are not, so check carefully before you buy.

Lights are also necessary, and come in a large variety of types, strengths and sizes. A light source is necessary for plants in the tank to photosynthesize and give the tank a more attractive appearance. Even if you plan to use plastic plants, the fish still require light, although here you can use a lower strength light source.

A hood is necessary to keep dust, dirt and unwanted materials out of the tank. Sometimes the hood can also help prevent evaporation. Another requirement is aquarium gravel. This will improve the aesthetics of the aquarium and is necessary if you plan to have real plants.

9. What is the general tone of this article?

    a. Formal

    b. Informal

    c. Technical

    d. Opinion

READING COMPREHENSION

10. Which of the following cannot be inferred?

   a. Gravel is good for aquarium plants.

   b. Fewer people have aquariums in their office than at home.

   c. The larger the tank, the larger the filter required.

   d. None of the above.

11. What evidence does the author provide to support their claim that aquarium lights are necessary?

   a. Plants require light.

   b. Fish and plants require light.

   c. The author does not provide evidence for this statement.

   d. Aquarium lights make the aquarium more attractive.

12. Which of the following is an opinion?

   a. Filter with a 3 to 5 times turn over rate per hour are required.

   b. Aquarium gravel improves the aesthetics of the aquarium.

   c. An aquarium hood keeps dust, dirt and unwanted materials out of the tank.

   d. Each type of tropical fish has its own ideal water temperature.

Questions 13 - 16 refer to the following passage.

The Civil War

The Civil War began on April 12, 1861. The first shots of the Civil War were fired in Fort Sumter, South Carolina. Note that even though more American lives were lost in the Civil

War than in any other war, not one person died on that first day. The war began because eleven Southern states seceded from the Union and tried to start their own government, The Confederate States of America.

Why did the states secede? The issue of slavery was a primary cause of the Civil War. The eleven southern states relied heavily on their slaves to foster their farming and plantation lifestyles. The northern states, many of whom had already abolished slavery, did not feel that the southern states should have slaves. The north wanted to free all the slaves and President Lincoln's goal was to both end slavery and preserve the Union. He had Congress declare war on the Confederacy on April 14, 1862. For four long, blood soaked years, the North and South fought.

From 1861 to mid 1863, it seemed as if the South would win this war. However, on July 1, 1863, an epic three day battle was waged on a field in Gettysburg, Pennsylvania. Gettysburg is remembered for being the bloodiest battle in American history. At the end of the three days, the North turned the tide of the war in their favor. The North then went on to dominate the South for the remainder of the war. A famous episode is General Sherman's "March to The Sea," where he famously led the Union Army through Georgia and the Carolinas, burning and destroying everything in their path.
In 1865, the Union army invaded and captured the Confederate capital of Richmond Virginia. Robert E. Lee, leader of the Confederacy surrendered to General Ulysses S. Grant, leader of the Union forces, on April 9, 1865. The Civil War was over and the Union was preserved.

13. What does secede mean?

    a. To break away from

    b. To accomplish

    c. To join

    d. To lose

14. Which of the following statements summarizes a FACT from the passage?

    a. Congress declared war and then the Battle of Fort Sumter began.

    b. Congress declared war after shots were fired at Fort Sumter.

    c. President Lincoln was pro slavery

    d. President Lincoln was at Fort Sumter with Congress

15. Which event finally led the Confederacy to surrender?

    a. The battle of Gettysburg

    b. The battle of Bull Run

    c. The invasion of the confederate capital of Richmond

    d. Sherman's March to the Sea

16. What does the word abolish as used in this passage mean?

    a. To ban

    b. To polish

    c. To support

    d. To destroy

Answer Key

1. A

We know that an annex is like an attic because the text states the annex was above Otto Frank's building.

Choice B is incorrect because an office building doesn't have bedrooms. Choice C is incorrect because a basement would be below the office building. Choice D is incorrect because there would not be a kitchen in an office building.

2. B

The diary has been published in 55 languages so people all over the world can learn about Anne. That is why the passage says it has been continuously in print.

Choice A is incorrect because it is too vague. Choice C is incorrect because it was published after Anne died and she did not write in all three languages. Choice D is incorrect because the passage does not give us any information about what languages Otto Frank spoke.

3. C

Use the process of elimination to figure this out.

Choice A cannot be the correct answer because otherwise the passage would have simply said that Anne and Margot both died of starvation. Choices B and D cannot be correct because if the Germans had done something specifically to murder Anne, the passage would have stated that directly. By the process of elimination, choice C has to be the correct answer.

4. D

We can figure this out using context clues. The paragraph is talking about Anne's diary and so, outlet in this instance is a place where Anne can pour her feelings.

Choice A is incorrect answer. That is the literal meaning of the word outlet and the passage is using the figurative meaning. Choice B is incorrect because that is the secondary literal meaning of the word outlet, as in an outlet mall. Again, we are looking for figurative meaning. Choice C is incorrect because

there are no clues in the text to support that answer.
5. B
When someone is avid about something that means they are highly interested in the subject. The context clues are dull and boring, because they define the opposite of avid.

6. A
The author is using a simile to compare the books to medicine. Medicine is what you take when you want to feel better. They are suggesting that if a person wants to feel good, they should read Dr. Seuss' books.

Choice B is incorrect because there is no mention of a doctor's office. Choice C is incorrect because it is using the literal meaning of medicine and the author is using medicine in a figurative way. Choice D is incorrect because it makes no sense. We know not to eat books.

7. D
The publisher is described as intelligent because he knew to get in touch with a famous author to develop a book that children would be interested in reading.

Choice A is incorrect because we can assume that all book publishers must know how to read. Choice B is incorrect because it says in the article that more than one publisher was concerned about whether or not children liked to read. Choice C is incorrect because there is no mention in the article about how well The Cat in the Hat sold when it was first published.

8. B
The passage describes in detail how Dr. Seuss had a great effect on the lives of children through his writing. It names several of his books, tells how he helped children become avid readers and explains his style of writing.

Choice A is incorrect because that is just one single fact about the passage. Choice C is incorrect because that is just one single fact about the passage. Choice D is incorrect because that is just one single fact about the passage. Again, choice B is correct because it encompasses ALL the facts in the passage, not just one single fact.

9. B
The general tone is informal.

10. B
The statement, "Fewer people have aquariums in their office than at home," cannot be inferred from this article.

11. B
Light is necessary for the fish and plants.

12. B
The following statement is an opinion, " Aquarium gravel improves the aesthetics of the aquarium."

13. A
Secede means to break away from because the 11 states wanted to leave the United States and form their own country.

Choice B is incorrect because the states were not accomplishing anything. Choice C is incorrect because the states were trying to leave the USA not join it. Choice D is incorrect because the states seceded before they lost the war.

14. B
Look at the dates in the passage. The shots were fired on April 12 and Congress declared war on April 14.

Choice C is incorrect because the passage states that Lincoln was against slavery. Choice D is incorrect because it never mentions who was or was not at Fort Sumter.

15. C
The passage states that Lee surrendered to Grant after the capture of the capital of the Confederacy, which is Richmond.

Choice A is incorrect because the war continued for 2 years after Gettysburg. Choice B is incorrect because that battle is not mentioned in the passage. Choice D is incorrect because the capture of the capital occurred after the march to the sea.

16. A

When the passage said that the North had *abolished* slavery, it implies that slaves were no longer allowed in the North. In essence slavery was banned.

Choice B makes no sense relative to the context of the passage. Choice C is incorrect because we know the North was fighting slavery, not for it. Choice D is incorrect because slavery is not a tangible thing that can be destroyed. It is a practice that had to be outlawed or banned.

Help with Reading Comprehension

At first sight, reading comprehension tests look challenging especially if you are given long essays to answer only two to three questions. While reading, you might notice your attention wandering, or you may feel sleepy. Do not be discouraged because there are various tactics and long-range strategies that make comprehending even long, boring essays easier.

Your friends before your foes. It is always best to start with passages with familiar subjects rather than those with unfamiliar ones. This approach applies the same logic as tackling easy questions before hard ones. Skip passages that do not interest you and leave them for later.

Don't use 'special' reading techniques. This is not the time for speed-reading or anything like that – just plain ordinary reading – not too slow and not too fast.

Read through the entire passage and the questions before you do anything. Many students try reading the questions first and then looking for answers in the passage thinking this approach is more efficient. What these students do not realize is that it is often hard to navigate in unfamiliar roads. If you do not familiarize yourself with the passage first, looking for answers become not only time-consuming but also dangerous because you might miss the context of the answer you are looking for. If you read the questions first you will only confuse yourself and lose valuable time.

Familiarize yourself with reading comprehension questions. If you are familiar with the common types of reading questions, you are able to take note of important parts of the passage, saving time. There are six major kinds of reading questions.

- **Main Idea**- Questions that ask for the central thought or significance of the passage.

- **Specific Details** - Questions that asks for explicitly stated ideas.

- **Drawing Inferences** - Questions that ask for a logical extension of statements.

- **Tone or Attitude** - Questions that test your ability to sense the emotional state of the author.

- **Context Meaning** – Questions that ask for the meaning of a word depending on the context.

- **Technique** – Questions that ask for the method of organization or the writing style of the author.

Read. Read. Read. The best preparation for reading comprehension tests is always to read, read and read. If you are not used to reading lengthy passages, you will probably lose concentration. Increase your attention span by making a habit out of reading. Read everyday and increase the time slowly each day.

Reading Comprehension tests become less daunting when you have trained yourself to read and understand fast. Always remember that it is easier to understand passages you are interested in. Do not read through passages hastily. Make mental notes of ideas you may be asked.

Reading Strategy

When facing the reading comprehension section of a standardized test, you need a strategy to be successful. You want to keep several steps in mind:

- **First, make a note of the time and the number of sections.** Time your work accordingly. Typically, four to five minutes per section is sufficient. Second, read the directions for each selection thoroughly before beginning (and listen carefully to any additional verbal instructions, as they will often clarify obscure or confusing written guidelines). You must know exactly how to do what you're about to do!

- **Now you're ready to begin reading the selection.** Read the passage carefully, noting significant characters or events on scrap paper or underlining on the test sheet. Many students find making a basic list in the margins helpful. Quickly jot down or underline one-word summaries of characters, notable happenings, numbers, or key ideas. This will help retain information and focus wandering thoughts. Remember, however, that your goal is to find the information that answers the questions. Even if you find the passage interesting, stay on track.

- **Now read the question and all the choices.** Now you have read the passage, have a general idea of the main ideas, and have marked the important points. Read the question and all the choices. Never choose an answer without reading them all! Questions are often designed to confuse – stay focussed and clear. Usually the answer choices will focus on one or two facts or inferences from the passage. Keep these clear in your mind.

- **Search for the answer.** With a very general idea of what the different choices are, go back to the passage and scan for the relevant information. Watch for big words, unusual or unique words. These make your job easier as you can scan the text for the particular word.

- **Mark the Answer.** Now you have the key information the question is looking for. Go back to the question, quickly scan the choices and mark the correct one.

Typically, there will be several questions dealing with facts from the selection, a couple more inference questions dealing with logical consequences of those facts, and periodically an application-oriented question surfaces to force you to make connections with what you already know. Some students prefer to answer the questions as listed, and feel classifying the question and then ordering is wasting precious time. Other students prefer to answer the different types of questions in order of how easy or difficult they are. The choice is yours and do whatever works for you. If you want to try answering in order of difficulty, here is a recommended order, answer fact questions first; they're easily found within the passage. Tackle inference problems next, after re-reading the question(s) as many times as you need to. Application or 'best guess' questions usually take the longest, so, save them for last.

Use the practice tests to try out both ways of answering and see what works for you.

For more help with reading comprehension, see Multiple Choice Secrets at www.multiple-choice.ca

Main Idea and Supporting Details

Identifying the main idea, topic and supporting details in a passage can feel like an overwhelming task. The passages used for standardized tests can be boring and seem difficult - Test writers don't use interesting passages or ones that talk about things most people are familiar with. Despite these obstacles, all passages and paragraphs will have the information you need to answer the questions.

The topic of a passage or paragraph is its subject. It's the general idea and can be summed up in a word or short phrase. Sometimes, there is a short description of the passage if it's taken from a longer work. Make sure you read the description as it might state the topic of the passage. If not, read the passage and ask yourself, "Who, or what is this about?" For example:

Over the years, school uniforms have been hotly debated. Arguments are made that students have the right to show individuality and express themselves by choosing their own clothes. However, this brings up social and academic issues. Some kids cannot afford to wear the clothes they like and might be bullied by the "better dressed" students. With attention drawn to clothes and the individual, students will lose focus on class work and the reason they are in school. School uniforms should be mandatory.

Ask: What is this paragraph about?

Topic: school uniforms

Once you have the topic, it's easier to find the main idea. The main idea is a specific statement telling what the writer wants you to know. Writers usually state the main idea as a thesis statement. If you're looking for the main idea of a single paragraph, the main idea is called the topic sentence and will probably be the first or last sentence. If you're looking for the main idea of an entire passage, look for the thesis statement in either the first or last paragraph. The main idea is usually restated in the conclusion. To find the main idea of a passage or paragraph, follow these steps:

1. Find the topic.

2. Ask yourself, "What point is the author trying to make about the topic?"

3. Create your own sentence summarizing the author's point.

4. Look in the text for the sentence closest in meaning to yours.

Look at the example paragraph again. It's already established that the topic of the paragraph is school uniforms. What is the main idea/topic sentence?

Reading Comprehension

Ask: "What point is the author trying to make about school uniforms?"

Summary: Students should wear school uniforms.

Topic sentence: School uniforms should be mandatory.

Main Idea: School uniforms should be mandatory.

Each paragraph offers supporting details to explain the main idea. The details could be facts or reasons, but they will always answer a question about the main idea. What? Where? Why? When? How? How much/many? Look at the example paragraph again. You'll notice that more than one sentence answers a question about the main idea. These are the supporting details.

Main Idea: School uniforms should be mandatory.

Ask: Why? Some kids cannot afford to wear clothes they like and could be bullied by the "better dressed" kids. Supporting Detail

With attention drawn to clothes and the individual, Students will lose focus on class work and the reason they are in school. Supporting Detail

What if the author doesn't state the main idea in a topic sentence? The passage will have an implied main idea. It's not as difficult to find as it might seem. Paragraphs are always organized around ideas. To find an implied main idea, you need to know the topic and then find the relationship between the supporting details. Ask yourself, "What is the point the author is making about the relationship between the details?"

> Cocoa is what makes chocolate good for you. Chocolate comes in many varieties. These delectable flavors include milk chocolate, dark chocolate, semi-sweet, and white chocolate.

Ask: What is this paragraph about?

Topic: Chocolate

Ask: What? Where? Why? When? How? How much/many?

Supporting details: Chocolate is good for you because it is made of cocoa, Chocolate is delicious, Chocolate comes in different delicious flavors

Ask: What is the relationship between the details and what is the author's point?

Main Idea: Chocolate is good because it is healthy and it tastes good.

Testing Tips for Main Idea Questions

1. Skim the questions – not the answer choices - before reading the passage.

2. Questions about main idea might use the words "theme," "generalization," or "purpose."

3. Save questions about the main idea for last. Questions can often be found in order in the passage.

3. Underline topic sentences in the passage. Most tests allow you to write in your test booklet.

4. Answer the question in your own words before looking at the answer choices. Then match your answer with an answer choice.

5. Cross out incorrect answer choices immediately to prevent confusion.

6. If two of the answer choices mean the same thing but use different words, they are BOTH incorrect.

7. If a question asks about the whole passage, cross out the answer choices that apply to only part of it.

8. If only part of the information is correct, that answer choice is incorrect.

9. An answer choice that is too broad is incorrect. All information needs to be backed up by the passage.

10. Answer choices with extreme wording are usually incorrect.

Drawing Inferences and Conclusions

Video Tutorial

https://www.test-preparation.ca/making-inferences-and-drawing-conclusions-video-tutorial/

Drawing inferences and making conclusions happens all the time. In fact, you probably do it every time you read—sometimes without even realizing it! For example, remember the first time that you saw the movie "The Lion King." When you meet Scar for the first time, he is trapping a helpless mouse with his sharp claws preparing to eat it. When you see this action you guess that Scar is going to be a bad character in the movie. Nothing appeared to tell you this. No caption came across the bottom of the screen that said "Bad Guy." No red arrow pointed to Scar and said "Evil Lion." No, you made an inference about his character based on the context clue you were given. You do the same thing when you read!

When you draw an inference or make a conclusion you are doing the same thing, you are making an educated guess based on the hints the author gives you. We call these hints "context clues." Scar trapping the innocent mouse is the context clue about Scar's character.

Usually you are making inferences and drawing conclusions the entire time that you are reading. Whether you realize it or not, you are constantly making educated guesses based on context clues. Think about a time you were reading a book and something happened that you were expecting to happen. You're not psychic! Actually, you were picking up on the context clues and making inferences about what was going to happen next!

Let's try an easy example. Read the following sentences and answer the questions at the end of the passage.

Shelly really likes to help people. She loves her job because she gets to help people every single day. However, Shelly has to work long hours and she can get called in the middle of the night for emergencies. She wears a white lab coat at work and usually she carries a stethoscope.

What is most likely Shelly's job?

    a. Musician
    b. Lawyer
    c. Doctor
    d. Teacher

This probably seemed easy. Drawing inferences isn't always this simple, but it is the same basic principle. How did you know Shelly was a doctor? She helps people, she works long hours, she wears a white lab coat, and she gets called in for emergencies at night. Context Clues! Nowhere in the paragraph did it say Shelly was a doctor, but you were able to draw that conclusion based on the information provided in the paragraph. This is how it's done!

There is a catch, though. Remember that when you draw inferences based on reading, you should only use the information given to you by the author. Sometimes it is easy for us to make conclusions based on knowledge that is already in our mind—but that can lead you to drawing an incorrect inference. For example, let's pretend there is a bully at your school named Brent. Now let's say you read a story and the main character's name is Brent. You could NOT infer that the character in the story is a bully just because his name is Brent. You should only use the information given to you by the author to avoid drawing the wrong conclusion.

Let's try another example. Read the passage below, and answer the question.

Social media is an extremely popular new form of connecting and communicating over the internet. Since Facebook's original launch in 2004, millions of people have joined in the social media craze. In fact, it is estimated that almost 75% of all internet users aged 18 and older use some form of social media. Facebook started at Harvard University as a way to get students connected. However, it quickly grew into a worldwide phenomenon and today, the founder of Facebook, Mark Zuckerberg has an estimated net worth of 28.5 billion dollars.

Facebook is not the only social media platform, though. Other sites such as Twitter, Instagram, and Snapchat have since been invented and are quickly becoming just as popular! Many social media users actually use more than one type of social media. Furthermore, most social media sites have created mobile apps that allow people to connect via social media virtually anywhere in the world!

What is the most likely reason that other social media sites like Twitter and Instagram were created?

a. Professors at Harvard University made it a class project.

b. Facebook was extremely popular and other people thought they could also be successful by designing social media sites.

c. Facebook was not connecting enough people.

d. Mark Zuckerberg paid people to invent new social media sites because he wanted lots of competition.

Here, the correct answer is B. Facebook was extremely popular and other people thought they could also be successful by designing social media sites. How do we know this? What are the context clues? Take a look at the first paragraph. What do we know based on this paragraph? Well, one sentence refers to Facebook's original launch. This suggests that Facebook was one of the first social media sites. In addition, we know that the founder of Facebook has been extremely successful and is worth billions of dollars. From this we can infer that other people wanted to imitate Facebook's idea and become just as successful as Mark Zuckerberg.

Let's go through the other answers. If you chose A, it might be because Facebook started at Harvard University, so you drew the conclusion that all other social media sites were also started at Harvard University. However, there is no mention of class projects, professors, or students designing social media. So there doesn't seem to be enough support for choice A.

If you chose C, you might have been drawing your own conclusions based on outside information. Maybe none of your friends are on Facebook, so you made an inference that Facebook didn't connect enough people, so more sites were invented. Or maybe you think the people who connect on Facebook are too old, so you don't think Facebook connects enough people your age. This might be true, but remember inferences should be drawn from the information the author gives you!

If you chose D, you might be using the information that Mark Zuckerberg is worth over 28 billion dollars. It would be easy for him to pay others to design new sites, but remember, you need to use context clues! He is very wealthy, but that statement was giving you information about how successful Facebook was—not suggesting that he paid others to design more sites!

So remember, drawing inferences and conclusions is simply about using the information you are given to make an educated guess. You do this every single day so don't let this concept scare you. Look for the context clues, make sure they support your claim, and you'll be able to make accurate inferences and conclusions!

Meaning From Context

Often in reading comprehension questions, you are asked for the definition of a word, which you have to infer from the surrounding text, called "meaning in context." Here are a few examples with step-by-step solutions, and a few tips and tricks to answering meaning from context questions.

There are literally thousands and thousands of words in the English language. It is impossible for us to know what every single one of them means, but we also don't have time to Google a definition every time we read a word we don't understand! Even the smartest person in the world comes across words they don't know, but luckily we can use context clues to help us determine what things actually mean.

Context clues are really just little hints that can help us determine the meaning of words or phrases and honestly, the easiest way to learn how to use context clues is to practice!

Let's start with a few basic examples.

> In some countries many people are not given access to schools, teachers, or books. In these countries, people might be illiterate.

You might not know what the word illiterate means, but let's use the clues in the sentence to help us. If people are not given access to schools, teachers, or books, what might happen? They probably don't learn what we learned in school so they might not know some of the things that we learned from our teachers! Illiterate actually means "unable to read or write." This makes sense based on the context clues!

Let's work through another example.

> We have so much technology today! So much technology that many people have started using tablets and computers to read ebooks instead of paper books! In fact, some of these people actually think that reading paper books is archaic!

Let's look for the context clues. Well, what do we know from this paragraph? We have a lot of technology and sometimes people read ebooks instead of paper books. From this we can draw the conclusion that ebooks are beginning to replace paper books because ebooks are newer and better. So if ebooks are newer and better, it must mean that paper books are older. Archaic actually means "very old or old-fashioned," which again we determined from the context clues.

Let's see if you can try a few on your own now.

> Cody noticed the strawberries in his refrigerator were old and moldy, so he abstained and threw them away.

What does abstained most likely mean?

   a. chose not to consume
   b. washed
   c. shared
   d. cut into pieces

The correct answer here is A. The context clues told you the strawberries were old and moldy and told you that Cody did something and then threw them away. If the strawberries were moldy, and Cody abstained, it makes sense that he didn't eat them—which is choice A.

You may have chosen answer B. If the strawberries were old and moldy, Cody could have washed them. But use ALL of the context clues. After he abstained, he threw them away. Why would Cody wash them and then throw them away? That doesn't make sense! In addition, why would he share them if they were old and moldy? Finally, I suppose Cody could have cut them into pieces, but why would he need to do that before throwing them away? It doesn't make as much sense, so choice A is the correct answer!

Reading Comprehension

Let's do one more.

Scott had a disdain for Lily ever since she lied to their boss and got him fired.

a. Compassion
b. Hate
c. Remorse
d. Money

The correct answer is B. Scott was fired because Lily lied. Can you imagine if this happened to you? I think you would have some pretty strong feelings just like Scott!

It's simple! By understanding the context, you can determine the meaning of even the hardest of words!

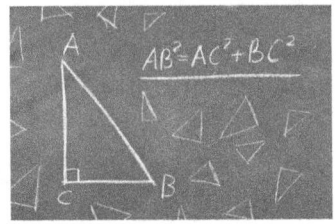

Mathematics & Problem Solving

THIS SECTION CONTAINS A SELF-ASSESSMENT AND MATH TUTORIALS. The Tutorials are designed to familiarize general principles and the Self-Assessment contains general questions similar to the math questions likely to be on the Ironworkers exam, but are not intended to be identical to the exam questions. The tutorials are not designed to be a complete math course, and it is assumed that students have some familiarity with math. If you do not understand parts of the tutorial, or find the tutorial difficult, it is recommended that you seek out additional instruction.

Tour of the Ironworkers Mathematics Content

The Ironworkers Test mathematics section has 50 questions. Below is a detailed list of the mathematics topics likely to appear on the Ironworkers Test. Make sure that you understand these topics at the very minimum.

- Convert decimals, percent, and fractions

- Solve word problems

MATHEMATICS

- Calculate percent and ratio

- Operations using fractions, percent and decimals

- Basic Geometry

- Basic Algebra

- Basic Geometry

- Understand and solve simple algebra problems

The questions in the self-assessment are not the same as you will find on the Ironworkers Test - that would be too easy! And nobody knows what the questions will be and they change all the time. Mostly, the changes consist of substituting new questions for old, but the changes also can be new question formats or styles, changes to the number of questions in each section, changes to the time limits for each section, and combining sections. So, while the format and exact wording of the questions may differ slightly, and changes from year to year, if you can answer the questions below, you will have no problem with the mathematics section of the Ironworkers Test.

MATHEMATICS SELF-ASSESSMENT

The purpose of the self-assessment is:

- Identify your strengths and weaknesses.

- Develop your personalized study plan (above)

- Get accustomed to the Ironworkers format

- Extra practice – the self-assessments are almost a full 3rd practice test!

- Provide a baseline score for preparing your study schedule.

Since this is a Self-assessment, and depending on how confident you are with mathematics, timing yourself is optional. The Ironworkers Test has 50 questions, to be answered in 60 minutes. This self-assessment has 30 questions, so allow about 35 minutes to complete.

Once complete, use the table below to assess your understanding of the content, and prepare your study schedule described in chapter 1.

80% - 100%	Excellent – you have mastered the content
60 – 79%	Good. You have a working knowledge. Even though you can just pass this section, you may want to review the Tutorials and do some extra practice to see if you can improve your mark.
40% - 59%	Below Average. You do not understand the content. Review the tutorials, and retake this quiz again in a few days, before proceeding to the rest of the Practice Test Questions.
Less than 40%	Poor. You have a very limited understanding. Please review the Tutorials, and retake this quiz again in a few days, before proceeding to the Practice Test Questions.

Mathematics

Math Self-Assessment

	A	B	C	D	E			A	B	C	D	E
1	○	○	○	○	○		21	○	○	○	○	○
2	○	○	○	○	○		22	○	○	○	○	○
3	○	○	○	○	○		23	○	○	○	○	○
4	○	○	○	○	○		24	○	○	○	○	○
5	○	○	○	○	○		25	○	○	○	○	○
6	○	○	○	○	○		26	○	○	○	○	○
7	○	○	○	○	○		27	○	○	○	○	○
8	○	○	○	○	○		28	○	○	○	○	○
9	○	○	○	○	○		29	○	○	○	○	○
10	○	○	○	○	○		30	○	○	○	○	○
11	○	○	○	○	○		31	○	○	○	○	○
12	○	○	○	○	○		32	○	○	○	○	○
13	○	○	○	○	○		33	○	○	○	○	○
14	○	○	○	○	○		34	○	○	○	○	○
15	○	○	○	○	○		35	○	○	○	○	○
16	○	○	○	○	○		36	○	○	○	○	○
17	○	○	○	○	○		37	○	○	○	○	○
18	○	○	○	○	○		38	○	○	○	○	○
19	○	○	○	○	○							
20	○	○	○	○	○							

Decimals, Fractions and Percent

1. 15 is what some oranges?

    a. 7.50%
    b. 15%
    c. 20%
    d. 17.50%

2. A boy has 5 red balls, 3 white balls and 2 yellow balls. What percent of the balls are yellow?

    a. 2%
    b. 8%
    c. 20%
    d. 12%

3. Add 10% of 300 to 50% of 20

    a. 50%
    b. 40%
    c. 60%
    d. 45%

4. Convert 75% to a fraction.

    a. 2/100
    b. 85/100
    c. 3/4
    d. 4/7

MATHEMATICS

5. Convert 90% to a fraction

    a. 1/10
    b. 9/9
    c. 10/100
    d. 9/10

6. Multiply 3 by 25% of 40

    a. 75
    b. 30
    c. 68
    d. 35

7. Convert 0.28 to a fraction.

    a. 7/25
    b. 3.25
    c. 8/25
    d. 5/28

8. Convert 0.45 to a fraction

    a. 7/20
    b. 7/45
    c. 9/20
    d. 3/20

9. Convert 1/5 to percent.

    a. 10%
    b. 5%
    c. 20%
    d. 25%

10. Convert 4/20 to percent

    a. 25%
    b. 20%
    c. 40%
    d. 30%

11. A man buys an item for $420 and has a balance of 3000.00. How much did he have before?

    a. $2,580
    b. $3,420
    c. $2,420
    d. $342

12. Divide 9.60 by 3.2

    a. 2.50
    b. 3
    c. 2.3
    d. 6.4

Basic Algebra

13. If X = 7 solve 3x + 5 − 2x

    a. x = 6
    b. x = 12
    c. x = 1
    d. x = 0

Mathematics

14. $(x - 2) / 4 - (3x + 5) / 7 = -3$, $x=?$

    a. 6
    b. 7
    c. 10
    d. 13

15. Estimate 5205 / 25

    a. 108
    b. 308
    c. 208
    d. 408

Exponents

16. Express in 3^4 standard form

    a. 81
    b. 27
    c. 12
    d. 9

17. Simplify $4^3 + 2^4$

    a. 45
    b. 108
    c. 80
    d. 48

18. If $x = 2$ and $y = 5$, solve $xy^3 - x^3$

    a. 240
    b. 258
    c. 248
    d. 242

19. $X^3 \times X^2$

   a. 5^x
   b. x^{-5}
   c. x^{-1}
   d. X^5

20. Express 100000^0 standard form

   a. 1
   b. 0
   c. 100000
   d. 1000

GEOMETRY

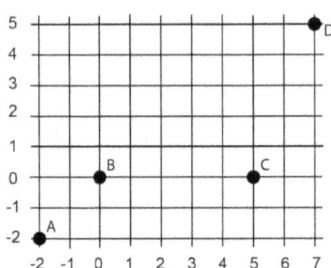

21. Which of the above points represents the origin?

   a. A
   b. B
   c. C
   d. D

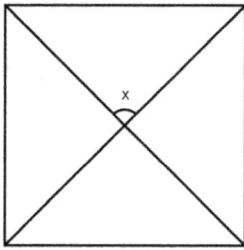

22. What is measurement of the indicated angle?

    a. 45°
    b. 90°
    c. 60°
    d. 30°

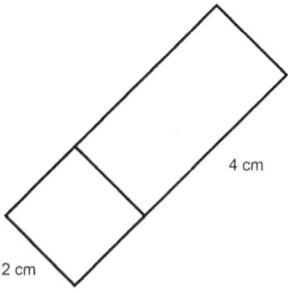

Note: figure not drawn to scale.

23. Assuming the figure with side 2 cm. is square, what is the perimeter of the above shape?

    a. 12 cm
    b. 16 cm
    c. 6 cm
    d. 20 cm

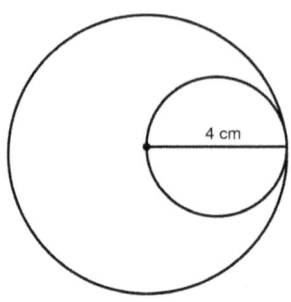

4 cm

Note: Figure not drawn to scale

24. Assuming the diameter of the small circle is the radius of the larger circle, what is (area of large circle) - (area of small circle) in the figure above?

    a. 8 π cm²
    b. 10 π cm²
    c. 12 π cm²
    d. 16 π cm²

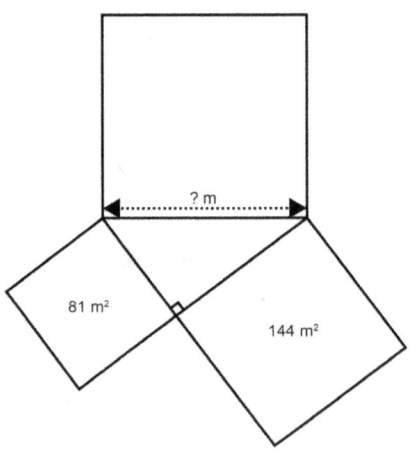

Note: Figure not drawn to scale

25. Assuming the shapes around the center right triangle are square, what is the length of each side of the indicated square above?

    a. 10
    b. 15
    c. 20
    d. 5

Problem Solving

26. The total expense of building a fence around a square-shaped field is $2000 at a rate of $5 per meter. What is the length of one side?

    a. 80 meters
    b. 100 meters
    c. 40 meters
    d. 320 meters

27. There are some oranges in a basket. By adding 8/5 of the total to the basket the new total became 130. How many oranges were in the basket?

    a. 50
    b. 60
    c. 40
    d. 35

28. A building is 15 m long and 20 m wide and 10 m high. What is the volume of the building?

    a 45 m^3
    b. 3,000 m^3
    c. 1500 m^3
    d. 300 m^3

29. Mr. Brown bought 5 cheese burgers, 3 drinks and 4 orders of fries for his family and a cookie pack for his dog. If the price of all single items is same at $1.30, and a 3.5% tax is added, what is the total cost of dinner?

    a. $17.00
    b. $16.90
    c. $17.49
    d. $16.00

30. 3 boys are asked to clean a surface that is 4 ft^2. If the portion is divided equally among the boys, what size will each of them clean?

    a. 1 ft 6 inches^2
    b. 14 inches^2
    c. 1 ft 2 inches^2
    d. . 1 ft^2 48 inches^2

31. A small business owner deposits $6000 in a savings account at a local bank. After 2 years, at 3% interest rate, what will be the interest earned?

    a. $6360
    b. $360
    c. $240
    d. $460

32. Adelle is making spaghetti. The recipe says that for 500 grams of spaghetti, she should add 0.75 grams of salt. However, she just wants 125 grams of spaghetti. Based on this information, how much salt should she use?

    a. 0.38 grams
    b. 0.75 grams
    c. 0.19 grams
    d. 0.25 grams

MATHEMATICS

CONVERSION

33. Convert 10 kg. to grams.

    a. 10,000 grams
    b. 1,000 grams
    c. 100 grams
    d. 10.11 grams

34. 1 gallon = _____ liter(s).

    a. 1
    b. 3.785
    c. 37.85
    d. 4.5

35. Convert 2.5 liters to milliliters.

    a. 1,050 ml.
    b. 2,500 ml.
    c. 2,050 ml.
    d. 1,500 ml.

36. Convert 210 mg. to grams.

    a. 0.21 mg.
    b. 2.1 g.
    c. 0.21 g.
    d. 2.12 g.

37. Convert 10 pounds to kilograms.

    a. 4.54 kg.

    b. 11.25 kg.

    c. 15 kg.

    d. 10.25 kg.

38. Convert 0.539 grams to milligrams.

    a. 539 g.

    b. 539 mg.

    c. 53.9 mg.

    d. 0.53 g.

Answer Key

Decimals, Percent and Fractions

1. A
15/200 = X/100 = 1500 = 200X = 15 = 2X = 7.5%

2. C
Total no. of balls = 10, no. of yellow balls = 2, answer = 2/10 X 100 = 20%

3. B
10% of 300 = 30 and 50% of 20 = 10 so 30 + 10 = 40.

4. C
75% = 75/100 = 3/4

5. D
90% = 90/100 = 9/10

6. B
25% of 40 = 10 and 10 x 3 = 30

7. A
0.28 = 28/100 = 7/25

8. C
0.45 = 45/100 = 9/20

9. C
1/5 X 100 = 20%

10. B
4/20 X 100 = 1/5 X 100 = 20%

11. B
(Amount Spent) $420 + $3000 (Balance) = $3420

12. B
9.60/3.2 = 3

13. B
X = 7, so 3x = 3 x 7 = 21, 2x = 2 x 7 = 14, so 21 + 5 - 14 = 26 - 14 = 12. Be careful, to perform the operations in the correct order - multiplication first, then addition and subtraction.

14. C
There are two fractions containing x and the denominators are different. First, let us find a common denominator to simplify the expression. The least common multiplier of 4 and 7 is 28. Then,
7(x – 2) / 28 – 4(3x + 5) / 28 = - 3.28 / 28 ... Since both sides are written on the denominator 28 now, we can eliminate them:
7(x – 2) – 4(3x + 5) = - 84
7x – 14 – 12x – 20 = - 84
- 5x = - 84 + 14 + 20
- 5x = - 50
x = 50/5

x = 10

15. C
The approximate answer to 5205 / 25 is 208.

EXPONENTS

16. A
3 x 3 x 3 x 3 = 81

17. C
(4 x 4 x 4) + (2 x 2 x 2 x 2) = 64 + 16 = 80

18. D
$2(5)^3 – (2)^3$ = 2(125) – 8 = 250 – 8 = 242

19. D
$X^3 \times X^2 = X^{3+2} = X^5$

20. A
Any value (except 0) raised to the power of 0 equals 1.

Mathematics

Geometry

21. A
Point A represents the origin.

22. A
The diagonals of a square intersect at right angles, so each angle measures 90° Half of that angle will be 45°

23. B
We see that there is a square with side 2 cm and a rectangle adjacent to it, with one side 2 cm (common side with the square) and the other side 4 cm. The perimeter of a shape is found by summing up all sides surrounding the shape, not adding the ones inside the shape. Three 2 cm sides from the square, and two 4 cm sides and one 2 cm side from the rectangle contribute the perimeter.

So, the perimeter of the shape is: 2 + 2 + 2 + 4 + 2 + 4 = 16 cm.

24. C
In the figure, we are given a large circle and a small circle inside it; with the diameter equal to the radius of the large one. The diameter of the small circle is 4 cm. This means that its radius is 2 cm. Since the diameter of the small circle is the radius of the large circle, the radius of the large circle is 4 cm. The area of a circle is calculated by: πr^2 where r is the radius.

Area of the small circle: $\pi(2)^2 = 4\pi$

Area of the large circle: $\pi(4)^2 = 16\pi$

The difference area is found by:

Area of the large circle - Area of the small circle = $16\pi - 4\pi = 12\pi$

25. B
We see that there are three squares forming a right triangle in the middle. Two of the squares have the areas 81 m² and 144 m². If we denote their sides a and b respectively:

$a^2 = 81$ and $b^2 = 144$. The length which is asked is the hypotenuse; a and b are the opposite and adjacent sides of the right angle. By using the Pythagorean Theorem, we can find the value of the asked side:

Pythagorean Theorem:

$(Hypotenuse)^2 = (Opposite\ Side)^2 + (Adjacent\ Side)^2$

$h^2 = a^2 + b^2$

$a^2 = 81$ and $b^2 = 144$ are given. So;

$h^2 = 81 + 144$

$h^2 = 225$

$h = 15$ m

Problem Solving

26. B
Total expense is $2000 and we are informed that $5 is spent per meter. Combining these two information, we know that the total length of the fence is 2000/5 = 400 meters.

The fence is built around a square-shaped field. If one side of the square is "a," the perimeter of the square is "4a." Here, the perimeter is equal to 400 meters. So,

400 = 4a

100 = a → this means that one side of the square is equal to 100 meters

27. A
Suppose oranges in the basket before = x
Then: X + 8x/5 = 130
5x + 8x = 650 (multiply both sides by 5)
13x = 650, x = 650/13
X = 50

28. D
Formula for volume of a shape is L x W x H = 15 x 20 x 10 = 3,000 m³

MATHEMATICS

29. C
The price of all the single items is same and there are 13 items. So the total cost will be 13 X 1.3 = $16.90. After the 3.5% tax, the total will be 16.9 X 1.035 = $17.49.

30. D
1 foot is equal to 12 inches. So 1 ft^2 = 12 * 12 in^2
4 ft^2 = 4 * 12 * 12 in^2 = 576 in^2

The total surface area is divided equally among 3 boys.

Each boy will clean 576/3 = 192 in^2

192 in^2 = 144 in^2 + 48 in^2; 144 in^2 = 1 ft^2

So, each boy will clean 1 ft^2 and 48 in^2

31. B
Interest (I) = ?, Rate (r) = 3%, Time (t) = 2 years, Principal (P) = 6000. Convert rate to decimal. 3% = 0.03. Then plug in variables into the simple interest formula. I = P x r x t, I = 6000 x 0.03 x 2, I = $360

32. C
125 : 500 is the same as 25 : 100 or 1 : 4. So the amount of salt will be 0.75/4 = 0.1875, or about .19 grams.

METRIC CONVERSION

33. A
1kg = 1,000 g and 10 kg = 10 x 1,000 = 10,000 g

34. B
1 US gallon = 3.78541178 liters

35. B
1 liter = 1,000 milliliters, 2.5 liters = 2.5 x 1,000 = 2,500 milliliters

36. C
1,000 mg = 1 g, 210 mg = 210/1000 = 0.21 g. Be careful of Choice A, (0.21 **mg.**) The numbers are the same but the units are different.

37. A
1 pound = 0.45 kg, 10 pounds = 4.53592, or about 4.54 kg. When multiplying a decimal by 10, move the decimal point one place to the left.

38. B
1 g = 1,000 mg. 0.539 g = 0.539 x 1000 = 539 mg.

Basic Math Video Tutorials

https://www.test-preparation.ca/basic-math-video-tutorials/

Fraction Tips, Tricks and Shortcuts

When you are writing an exam, time is precious, so anything you can do to answer questions faster is a real advantage.

Here are some ideas, shortcuts, tips and tricks that can speed up answering fraction problems.

Remember that a fraction is just a number which names a portion of something. For instance, instead of having a whole pie, a fraction says you have a part of a pie--such as a half of one or a fourth of one.

Two numbers make up a fraction. The number on top is the numerator. The number on the bottom is the denominator.

To remember which is which, just remember that "denominator" and "down" both start with a "d." And the "downstairs" number is the denominator. So for instance, in ½, the numerator is 1, and the denominator (or "downstairs") number is 2.

Adding Fractions

It's easy to add two fractions if they have the same denominator. Just add the digits on top and leave the bottom one the same: 1/10 + 6/10 = 7/10.

It's the same with subtracting fractions with the same denominator: 7/10 - 6/10 = 1/10.

Adding and subtracting fractions with different denominators is a little more complicated.

First, you have to arrange the fractions so they have the same denominators.

The easiest way to do this is to multiply the denominators: For 2/5 + 1/2 multiply 5 by 2. Now you have a denominator of 10.

But now you have to change the top numbers too. Since you multiplied the 5 in 2/5 by 2, you also multiply the 2 by 2, to get 4. So the first fraction is now 4/10.

In the second fraction, you multiplied the denominator by 5, you have to multiply the numerator by 5 also, to get 5/10.

Now you have 4/10 + 5/10 and you can add 5 and 4 to get 9/10.

Simplest Form

To reduce a fraction to its simplest form, you have to arrange the numerator and denominator so the only common factor is 1.

Think of it this way:

Let's take an example: The fraction 2/10.

This is not reduced to its simplest terms because there is a number that will divide evenly into both: 2. We want to make it so that the only number that will divide evenly into both is 1.
Divide the top and bottom by 2 to get the new, reduced fraction - 1/5.

Mathematics

Multiplying Fractions

This is the easiest of all: Just multiply the two top numbers and then multiply the two bottom numbers.

Here is an example,

2/5 X 2/3

First, multiply the numerators: 2 X 2 = 4

then multiply the denominators: 5 X 3 = 15

Your answer is 4/15.

Dividing Fractions

Dividing fractions is easy if you remember a simple trick - first turn the second fraction upside down - then multiply!

Here is an example:

7/8 X 1/2

Turn the second fraction upside down:

7/8 X 2/1

then multiply:

(7 X 2) / (8 X 1) = 14/8

Converting Fractions to Decimals

There are a couple of ways to convert fractions to decimals. The first, which is the fastest -- is to memorize some basic fraction facts.

1/100 is "one hundredth," expressed as a decimal, it's .01.

1/50 is "two hundredths," expressed as a decimal, it's .02.

1/25 is "one twenty-fifth" or "four hundredths," expressed as a decimal, it's .04.

1/20 is "one twentieth" or ""five hundredths," expressed as a decimal, it's .05.

1/10 is "one tenth," expressed as a decimal, it's .1.

1/8 is "one eighth," or "one hundred twenty-five thousandths," expressed as a decimal, it's .125.

1/5 is "one fifth," or "two tenths," expressed as a decimal, it's .2.

1/4 is "one fourth" or "twenty-five hundredths," expressed as a decimal, it's .25.

1/3 is "one third" or "thirty-three hundredths," expressed as a decimal, it's .33.

1/2 is "one half" or "five tenths," expressed as a decimal, it's .5.

3/4 is "three fourths," or "seventy-five hundredths," expressed as a decimal, it's .75.

Of course, if you're no good at memorization, another good technique for converting a fraction to a decimal is to manipulate it so that the fraction's denominator is 10, 100, 1000, or some other power of 10.

MATHEMATICS   71

Here's an example: We'll start with three quarters. What is the first number in the 4 "times table" that you can multiply and get a multiple of 10? Can you multiply 4 by something to get 10? No. Can you multiply it by something to get 100? Yes! 4 X 25 is 100.

So multiply the numerator by 25, which is 75 over 100

We know fractions are really a division problem, and we also know that dividing by 100, means we move the decimal 2 places to the left.

So, 75 over 100 = .75

Lets try another example - Convert one fifth to a decimal.

First find a power of 10 that 5 goes into evenly, which is 2.

Multiply the numerator and denominator by 2, which is

two tenths.

Dividing 2 by 10 means we move the decimal place 1 place to the left.

So 1/5 = 0.5

CONVERTING FRACTIONS TO PERCENT

Here is a quick method to convert fraction to percent and a strategy for answering on a multiple choice test that will save you valuable exam time.

First, remember that a fraction is a division problem: you're dividing the bottom number into the top.

Taking an example, convert 2/3 into percent.

The first method is to multiple the numerator by 100 and divide. So,

(2 X 100) / 2 = 100/3 = 66.66

Add a % sign and you have the answer, 66.66%

If you're doing these conversions on a multiple-choice test, here's an idea that might be even easier and faster. Let's say you have a fraction of 1/8 and you're asked to convert to percent.

Since we know that "percent" means hundredths, ask yourself what number we can multiply 8 by to get 100. Since there is no number, ask what number gets us close to 100.

That number is 12: 8 X 12 = 96. So it gets us a little less than 100. Now, whatever you do to the denominator, you have to do to the numerator. Let's multiply 1 X 12 and we get 12. However, since 96 is a little less than 100, we know that our answer will be a little MORE than 12%.

Look at the choices and eliminate the obvious wrong choices. So if your possible answers on the multiple-choice test are these:

a) 8.5% b) 19% c) 12.5% d) 25%

then we know the answer is c) 12.5%, because it's a little MORE than the 12 we got in our math problem above.

Here all the choices except choice C 12.5% can be eliminated.

You don't have to know the exact correct answer, just enough to estimate, then eliminate the obviously wrong answers.

This was an easy example to demonstrate the strategy, but don't be fooled! You probably won't get such an easy question on your exam. By estimating your answer quickly, then eliminating obviously incorrect choices immediately, you save precious exam time.

MATHEMATICS

Decimal Tips, Tricks and Shortcuts

Converting Decimals to Fractions

Converting decimals to fractions is easy if you say it the right way! If you say "point one" or "point 25," you'll have trouble.

But if you say, "one tenth" and "twenty-five hundredths," then you have already solved it! That's because, if you know your fractions, you know that "one tenth" looks like this: 1/10. And "twenty-five hundredths" looks like this: 25/100.

Even if you have digits before the decimal, such as 3.4, learning how to say the word will help you with the conversion into a fraction. It's not "three point four," it's "three and four tenths." Knowing this, you know that the fraction which looks like "three and four tenths" is 3 4/10.

The conversion is not complete until you reduce the fraction to its lowest terms: It's not 25/100, but 1/4.

Converting Decimals to Percent

Changing a decimal to a percent is easy if you remember one thing: multiply by 100.

For example, if you start with .45, simply multiply it by 100 for 45. Then add the % sign to the end - 45%.

Think of it this way: take out the decimal point, add a percent sign on the opposite side. In other words, the decimal on the left is replaced by the % on the right.

It doesn't work quite that easily if the decimal is in the middle of the number. For example, 3.7. Here, take out the decimal in the middle and replace it with a 0 % at the end.

So 3.7 converted to decimal is 370%.

Percent Tips, Tricks and Shortcuts

Percent problems are not nearly as scary as they appear, if you remember this neat trick:

Draw a cross as in:

Portion	Percent
Whole	100

In the upper left, write PORTION. In the bottom left write WHOLE. In the top right, write PERCENT and in the bottom right, write 100. Whatever your problem is, you will leave blank the unknown, and fill in the other four parts. For example, let's suppose your problem is: Find 10% of 50. Since we know the 10% part, we put 10 in the percent corner. Since the whole number in our problem is 50, we put that in the corner marked whole. You always put 100 underneath the percent, so we leave it as is, which leaves only the top left corner blank. This is where we'll put our answer. Now simply multiply the two corner numbers that are NOT 100. Here, it's 10 X 50. That gives us 500. Now divide this by the remaining corner, or 100, to get a final answer of 5. 5 is the number that goes in the upper-left corner, and is your final solution.

Another hint to remember: Percents are the same thing as hundredths in decimals. So .45 is the same as 45 hundredths or 45 percent.

MATHEMATICS

Converting Percents to Decimals

Percents are just a type of decimal, so it should be no surprise that converting between the two is actually fairly simple. Here are a few tricks and shortcuts to keep in mind:

- Remember that percent literally means "per 100" or "for every 100." So when you speak of 30% you're saying 30 for every 100 or the fraction 30/100. In basic math, you learned that fractions that have 10 or 100 as the denominator can easily be turned to a decimal. 30/100 is thirty hundredths, or expressed as a decimal, .30.
- Another way to look at it: To convert a percent to a decimal, simply divide the number by 100. So for instance, if the percent is 47%, divide 47 by 100. The result will be .47. Get rid of the % mark and you're done.
- Remember that the easiest way of dividing by 100 is by moving your decimal two spots to the left.

Converting Percents to Fractions

Converting percents to fractions is easy. After all, a percent is just a type of fraction; it tells you what part of 100 that you're talking about. Here are some simple ideas for making the conversion from a percent to a fraction:

- If the percent is a whole number -- say 34% -- then simply write a fraction with 100 as the denominator (the bottom number). Then put the percentage itself on top. So 34% becomes 34/100.
- Now reduce as you would reduce any percent. In this case, by dividing 2 into 34 and 2 into 100, you get 17/50.
- If your percent is not a whole number -- say 3.4% --then convert it to a decimal expressed as hundredths. 3.4 is the same as 3.40 (or 3 and forty hundredths). Now ask yourself how you would express "three and forty hundredths" as a fraction. It would, of course, be 3 40/100. Reduce this and it becomes 3 2/5.

Exponents – A Quick Tutorial

Exponents seem like advanced math to most—like some mysterious code with a complicated meaning. In fact, though, an exponent is just short hand for saying that you're multiplying a number by itself two or more times. For instance, instead of saying that you're multiplying 5 x 5 x 5, you can show that you're multiplying 5 by itself 3 times if you just write 5^3. We usually say this as "five to the third power" or "five to the power of three." In this example, the raised 3 is an "exponent," while the 5 is the "base." You can even use exponents with fractions. For instance, $1/2^3$ means you're multiplying 1/2 x 1/2 x 1/2. (The answer is 1/8). Some other helpful hints for working with exponents:

- Here's how to do basic multiplication of exponents. If you have the same number with a different exponent (For instance 5^3 X 5^2) just add the exponents and multiply the bases as usual. The answer, then, is 25^5.
- This doesn't work, though, if the bases are different. For instance, in 5^3 X 3^2 we simply have to do the math the long way to figure out the final solution: 5 x 5 x 5, multiplying that result times the result for 3 X 3. (The answer is 1125).
- Looking at it from the opposite side, to divide two exponents with the same base (or bottom number), subtract the smaller exponent from the larger one. If we were dividing the problem above, we would subtract the 2 from the 3 to get 1. 5 to the power of 1 is simply 5.
- One time when thinking of exponents as merely multiplication doesn't work is when the raised number is zero. Any number raised to the "zeroth" power is 1 (Not, as we tend to think, zero).

Number (x)	x^2	x^3
1	1	1
2	4	8
3	9	27
4	16	64
5	25	125
6	36	216
7	49	343
8	64	512
9	81	729
10	100	1000
11	121	1331
12	144	1728
13	169	2197
14	196	2744
15	225	3375
16	256	4096

The time allowed on the math portion of a standardized test is typically so short that there's no room for error. You have to be fast and accurate.

Math strategy is very helpful, but nothing beats knowing your stuff! Make sure that you have learned all the important formulas that will be used.

If you don't know the formulas, strategy won't help you.

How to Answer Basic Math Questions - the Basics

First, read the problem, but not the answers.

Work through the problem first and come up with your own answers. Hopefully, you should find your answer among the choices.

If no answer matches the one you got, re-check your math, but this time, use a different method. In math, there are different ways to solve a problem.

Math Multiple Choice Strategy

The two strategies for working with basic math multiple choice are Estimation and Elimination.

Estimation is just as it sounds - try to estimate an approximate answer first. Then look at the choices.

Elimination is probably the most powerful strategy for answering multiple choice.

Eliminate obviously incorrect answers and narrowing the possible choices.

Here are a few basic math examples of how this works.

Solve 2/3 + 5/12

    a. 9/17
    b. 3/11
    c. 7/12
    d. 1 1/12

First estimate the answer. 2/3 is more than half and 5/12 is about half, so the answer is going to be very close to 1.

Next, Eliminate. Choice A is about 1/2 and can be eliminated, choice B is very small, less than 1/2 and can be eliminated. Choice C is close to 1/2 and can be eliminated. Leaving only choice D, which is just over 1.

Work through the solution, find a common denominator and add. The correct answer is 1 1/12, so Choice D is correct.

Let's look at another example:

Solve 4/5 – 2/3

   a. 2/2
   b. 2/13
   c. 1
   d. 2/15

First, quickly estimate the answer. 4/5 is very close to 1, and 2/3 more than half, so the answer is going to be less than 1/2.

Choice A can be eliminated right away, because it is 1. Choice C can be eliminated for the same reason.

Next, look at the denominators. Since 5 and 3 don't go into 13, choice B can be eliminated as well.

That leaves choice D. Checking the answer, the common denominator will be 15. So the answer is 2/15 and choice D is correct.

FRACTIONS SHORTCUT - CANCELLING OUT.

In any operation with fractions, if the numerator of one fractions has a common multiple with the denominator of the other, you can cancel out. This saves time, and simplifies the problem quickly, making it easier to manage.

Solve 2/15 ÷ 4/5

    a. 6/65

    b. 6/75

    c. 5/12

    d. 1/6

To divide fractions, we multiply the first fraction with the inverse of the second fraction. Therefore we have 2/15 x 5/4. The numerator of the first fraction, 2, shares a multiple with the denominator of the second fraction, 4, which is 2. These cancel out, which gives, 1/3 x 1/2 = 1/6

Cancelling out solved the questions very quickly, but we can still use multiple choice strategies to answer.

Choice B can be eliminated because 75 is too large a denominator. Choice C can be eliminated because 5 and 15 don't go into 12.

Choice D is correct.

Decimal Multiple Choice Strategy and Shortcuts.

Multiplying decimals gives a very quick way to estimate and eliminate choices. Anytime that you multiply decimals, it is going to give an answer with the same number of decimal places as the combined operands.

So for example,

2.38 X 1.2 will produce a number with three places of decimal, which is 2.856.

Here are a few examples with step-by-step explanation:

Solve 2.06 x 1.2

    a. 24.82

    b. 2.482

    c. 24.72

    d. 2.472

This is a simple question, but even before you start calculating, you can eliminate several choices. When multiplying decimals, there will always be as many numbers behind the decimal place in the answer as the sum of the ones in the initial problem, so choices A and C can be eliminated.

The correct answer is D: 2.06 x 1.2 = 2.472

Solve 20.0 ÷ 2.5

    a. 12.05

    b. 9.25

    c. 8.3

    d. 8

First estimate the answer to be around 10, and eliminate choice A. And since it'd also be an even number, you can eliminate Choices B and C, leaving only choice D.

The correct answer is choice D: 20.0 ÷ 2.5 = 8

Problem Solving

Do you know what the biggest tip for solving word problems is?

Practice regularly and systematically.

Sounds simple and easy right? Yes it is, and yes it really does work.

Word problems are a way of thinking and require you to translate a real-world problem into mathematical terms.

Some math teachers say that learning how to think mathematically is the main reason for teaching word problems.

So what does that mean?

Studying word problems and math in general requires a logical and mathematical frame of mind. The only way that you can get this is by practicing regularly, which means every day.

It is critical that you practice word problems every day for the 5 days before the exam as the absolute minimum.

If you practice and miss a day, you have lost the mathematical frame of mind and the benefit of your previous practice is gone. You must start all over again.

Everything is important.

All the information given in the problem has some purpose. There is no unnecessary information! Word problems are typically around 50 words in 2 or 3 sentences.

Often, the relationships are complicated. To explain everything, every word counts.

Make sure that you use every piece of information.

MATHEMATICS

7 STEPS TO SOLVING PROBLEMS

Step 1 – Read through the problem at least three times. The first reading should be a quick scan, and the next two readings should be done slowly to find answers to these questions:

> What does the problem ask? (Usually located at the end)

Mark all information and underline all important words or phrases.

Step 2 – Draw a picture. Use arrows, circles, lines, whatever works for you. This makes the problem real.

A favorite word problem is something like, 1 train leaves Station A travelling at 100 km/hr and another train leaves Station B travelling at 60 km/hr. ...

Draw a line, the two stations, and the two trains at either end.

Depending on the question, make a table with a blank portion to show information you don't know.

Step 3 – Assign a single letter to represent each unknown.

You may want to note the unknown that each letter represents so you don't get confused.

Step 4 – Translate the information into an equation.

Remember that the main problem with word problems is that they are not expressed in regular math equations. Your ability to identify correctly the variables and translate the information into an equation determines your ability to solve the problem.

Step 5 – Check the equation to see if it looks like regular equations that you are used to seeing and whether it looks sensible.

Does the equation appear to represent the information in the question? Take note that you may need to rewrite some formulas needed to solve the word problem equation.

Step 6 – Use algebra rules to solve the equation.

Simplify each side of the equation by removing parentheses and combining like terms.

Use addition or subtraction to isolate the variable term on one side of the equation. If a number crosses to the other side of the equation, the sign changes to the opposite -- for example positive to negative.

Use multiplication or division to solve for the variable. What you to once side of the equation you must do for the other.

Where there are multiple unknowns you will need to use elimination or substitution methods to resolve all the equations.

Step 7 – Check your final answers to see if they make sense with the information given in the problem.

For example, if the word problem involves a discount, the final price should be less or if a product was taxed then the final answer has to cost more.

Types of Problems

Word problems can be classified into 12 types. Below are examples of each type with a complete solution. Some types of word problems can be solved quickly using multiple choice strategies and some cannot. Always look for ways to estimate the answer and then eliminate choices.

1. Age

A girl is 10 years older than her brother. By next year, she will be twice the age of her brother. What are their ages now?

    a. 25, 15
    b. 19, 9
    c. 21, 11
    d. 29, 19

Solution: B

We will assume that the girl's age is "a" and her brother's age is "b." This means that based on the information in the first sentence,
$a = 10 + b$

Next year, she will be twice her brother's age, which gives, $a + 1 = 2(b + 1)$

We need to solve for one unknown factor and then use the answer to solve for the other. To do this we substitute the value of "a" from the first equation into the second equation. This gives

$10 + b + 1 = 2b + 2$
$11 + b = 2b + 2$
$11 - 2 = 2b - b$
$b = 9$

$9 = b$ this means that her brother is 9 years old. Solving for the girl's age in the first equation gives $a = 10 + 9$. $a = 19$ the girl is aged 19. So, the girl is aged 19 and the boy is 9

2. Distance or speed

Two boats travel down a river towards the same destination, starting at the same time. One boat is traveling at 52 km/hr, and the other boat at 43 km/hr. How far apart will they be after 40 minutes?

a. 46.67 km
b. 19.23 km
c. 6.04 km
d. 14.39 km

Solution: C

After 40 minutes, the first boat will have traveled = 52 km/hr x 40 minutes/60 minutes = 34.66 km
After 40 minutes, the second boat will have traveled = 43 km/hr x 40/60 minutes = 28.66 km
Difference between the two boats will be 34.66 km – 28.66 km = 6 km.

Multiple Choice Strategy

First estimate the answer. The first boat is travelling 9 km. faster than the second, for 40 minutes, which is 2/3 of an hour. 2/3 of 9 = 6, as a rough guess of the distance apart.

Choices A, B and D can be eliminated right away.

3. Ratio

The instructions in a cookbook state that 700 grams of flour must be mixed in 100 ml of water, and 0.90 grams of salt added. A cook however has just 325 grams of flour. What is the quantity of water and salt that he should use?

a. 0.41 grams and 46.4 ml
b. 0.45 grams and 49.3 ml
c. 0.39 grams and 39.8 ml
d. 0.25 grams and 40.1 ml

Solution: A

The Cookbook states 700 grams of flour, but the cook only has 325. The first step is to determine the percentage of flour he has 325/700 x 100 = 46.4%
That means that 46.4% of all other items must also be used.
46.4% of 100 = 46.4 ml of water
46.4% of 0.90 = 0.41 grams of salt.

Multiple Choice Strategy

The recipe calls for 700 grams of flour but the cook only has 325, which is just less than half, the quantity of water and salt are going to be about half.

Choices C and D can be eliminated right away. Choice B is very close so be careful. Looking closely at Choice B, it is exactly half, and since 325 is slightly less than half of 700, it can't be correct.

Choice A is correct.

4. Percent

An agent received $6,685 as his commission for selling a property. If his commission was 13% of the selling price, how much was the property?

    a. $68,825
    b. $121,850
    c. $49,025
    d. $51,423

Solution: D

Let's assume that the property price is x
That means from the information given, 13% of x = 6,685
Solve for x,
x = 6685 x 100/13 = $51,423

Multiple Choice Strategy

The commission, 13%, is just over 10%, which is easier to work with. Round up $6685 to $6700, and multiple by 10 for an approximate answer. 10 X 6700 = $67,000. You can do this in your head. Choice B is much too big and can be eliminated. Choice C is too small and can be eliminated. Choices A and D are left and good possibilities.

Do the calculations to make the final choice.

5. Sales & Profit

A store owner buys merchandise for $21,045. He transports them for $3,905 and pays his staff $1,450 to stock the merchandise on his shelves. If he does not incur further costs, how much does he need to sell the items to make $5,000 profit?

    a. $32,500
    b. $29,350
    c. $32,400
    d. $31,400

Solution: D

Total cost of the items is $21,045 + $3,905 + $1,450 = $26,400
Total cost is now $26,400 + $5000 profit = $31,400

Multiple Choice Strategy

Round off and add the numbers up in your head quickly. 21,000 + 4,000 + 1500 = 26500. Add in 5000 profit for a total of 31500.

Choice B is too small and can be eliminated. Choices C and A are too large and can be eliminated.

6. Tax/Income

A woman earns $42,000 per month and pays 5% tax on her monthly income. If the Government increases her monthly taxes by $1,500, what is her income after tax?

    a. $38,400
    b. $36,050
    c. $40,500
    d. $39, 500

Solution: A

Initial tax on income was 5/100 x 42,000 = $2,100

$1,500 was added to the tax to give $2,100 + 1,500 = $3,600
Income after tax is $42,000 - $3,600 = $38,400

7. Simple Interest Word Problems

Simple interest is one type of interest problems. There are always four variables of any simple interest equation. With simple interest, you would be given three of these variables and be asked to solve for one unknown variable. With more complex interest problems, you would have to solve for multiple variables.

The four variables of simple interest are:
P – Principal which refers to the original amount of money put in the account
I – Interest or the amount of money earned as interest
r – Rate or interest rate. This MUST ALWAYS be in decimal format and not in percentage
t – Time or the amount of time the money is kept in the account to earn interest

The formula for simple interest is I = P x r x t

Example 1

A customer deposits $1,000 in a savings account with a bank that offers 2% interest. How much interest will be earned after 4 years?
For this problem, there are 3 variables as expected.

P = $1,000
t = 4 years
r = 2%
I = ?

Before we can begin solving for I using the simple interest formula, we need to first convert the rate from percentage to decimal.

2% = 2/100 = 0.02

Now we can use the formula: I = P x r x t

I = 1,000 x 0.02 x 4 = 80
This means that the $1,000 would have earned an interest of $80 after 4 years. The total in the account after 4 years will thus be principal + interest earned, or 1,000 + 80 = $1,080

Example 2

Sandra deposits $1400 in a savings account with a bank at 5% interest. How long will she have to leave the money in the bank to earn $420 as interest to buy a second-hand car?

In this example, the given information is:
I = $420
P = $1,400
r - 5%
t - ?
As usual, first we convert the rate from percentage to decimal
5% = 5/100 = 0.05

Next, we plug in the variables we know into the simple interest formula - I = P x r x t

420 = 1,400 x 0.05 x t
420 = 70 x t
420 = 70t
t = 420/70
t = 6
Sandra will have to leave her $1,400 in the bank for 6 years to earn her an interest of $420 at a rate of 5%.

Other important simple interest formula to remember

To use this formula below, do not convert r (rate) to decimal.

P = 100 x interest/ r x t
r = 100 x interest/p x t
t = 100 x interest/ p x r

8. Averaging

The average weight of 10 books is 54 grams. 2 more books were added and the average weight became 55.4. If one of the 2 new books added weighed 62.8 g, what is the weight of the other?

    a. 44.7 g
    b. 67.4 g
    c. 62 g
    d. 52 g

Solution: C

Total weight of 10 books with average 54 grams will be = 10 × 54 = 540 g
Total weight of 12 books with average 55.4 will be = 55.4 × 12 = 664.8 g
So total weight of the remaining 2 will be= 664.8 – 540 = 124.8 g
If one weighs 62.8, the weight of the other will be= 124.8 g – 62.8 g = 62 g

Multiple Choice Strategy

Averaging problems can be estimated by looking at which direction the average goes. If additional items are added and the average goes up, the new items much be greater than the average. If the average goes down after new items are added, the new items must be less than the average.

Here, the average is 54 grams and 2 books are added which increases the average to 55.4, so the new books must weight more than 54 grams.
Choices A and D can be eliminated right away.

9. Probability

A bag contains 15 marbles of various colors. If 3 marbles are white, 5 are red and the rest are black, what is the probability of randomly picking out a black marble from the bag?

    a. 7/15
    b. 3/15
    c. 1/5
    d. 4/15

Solution: A

Total marbles = 15
Number of black marbles = 15 − (3 + 5) = 7
Probability of picking out a black marble = 7/15

10. Two Variables

A company paid a total of $2850 to book for 6 single rooms and 4 double rooms in a hotel for one night. Another company paid $3185 to book for 13 single rooms for one night in the same hotel. What is the cost for single and double rooms in that hotel?

    a. single= $250 and double = $345
    b. single= $254 and double = $350
    c. single = $245 and double = $305
    d. single = $245 and double = $345

Solution: D

We can determine the price of single rooms from the information given of the second company. 13 single rooms = 3185.
One single room = 3185 / 13 = 245
The first company paid for 6 single rooms at $245. 245 x 6 = $1470
Total amount paid for 4 double rooms by first company = $2850 - $1470 = $1380
Cost per double room = 1380 / 4 = $345

11. Geometry

The length of a rectangle is 5 in. more than its width. The perimeter of the rectangle is 26 in. What is the width and length of the rectangle?

    a. width = 6 inches, Length = 9 inches
    b. width = 4 inches, Length = 9 inches
    c. width = 4 inches, Length = 5 inches
    d. width = 6 inches, Length = 11 inches

Solution: B

Formula for perimeter of a rectangle is $2(L + W)$
p=26, so $2(L+W) = p$
The length is 5 inches more than the width, so
$2(w+5) + 2w = 26$
$2w + 10 + 2w = 26$
$2w + 2w = 26 - 10$
$4w = 16$

$W = 16/4 = 4$ inches

L is 5 inches more than w, so $L = 5 + 4 = 9$ inches.

12. Totals and fractions

A basket contains 125 oranges, mangos and apples. If 3/5 of the fruits in the basket are mangos and only 2/5 of the mangos are ripe, how many ripe mangos are there in the basket?

    a. 30
    b. 68
    c. 55
    d. 47

Solution: A
Number of mangos in the basket is 3/5 x 125 = 75
Number of ripe mangos = 2/5 x 75 = 30

Algebraic Equations

Algebra is a basic form of mathematics designed to define unknown quantities called variables. Variables in algebra are represented by letters, often x, y and z or a, b and c, and they are placed in equations alongside known quantities. An algebraic equation can be as simple as 2x=6 where simple division can tell us that x=6/2 or x = 3. Equations can also have variables on both sides such as 2x+3=8x. For this equation, we need to take more steps. First, subtracting 2x from both sides we get the equation 3=6x. From there it is again a simple matter of division to show that x=.5. The point of an equation is that it demonstrates that two distinct pieces of information have the same value. (It equates them.) Even though we do not know what 2x+3 is or what 8x is, we at least know that they are the same.

There are three types of equalities in algebra. There are reflexive equalities that say x=x. There are symmetric equalities that say that if x=y then y=x as well. And there are transitive equalities that say that if x=y and y=z then x=z.

The definite number next to the variable in each equation is called its coefficient. A variable can always be thought of as having a coefficient; if there is no number next to it, the coefficient equals 1, and if it has a negative sign in front of it, the coefficient equals -1.

Often, algebra is presented as word problems and it is up to you to figure out the equation. For instance, a question might describe a hockey team that has 6 wins, 3 losses in regulation time and 1 loss in overtime over their last 10 games. It will then tell you that the team has 13 points (awarded for wins and overtime losses to organize the league's standings) in their last 10 games and ask, given that a regulation loss earns a team 0 points: How many points is a win worth? How many is an overtime loss worth?

This question will give you the variables x = a win, y = a regulation loss and z = an overtime loss, from which you can derive the equation 6x+3y+1z=13. Since you already know that y=0 points, you can rewrite the equation as 6x+z=13. Now we have a two variable or polynomial equation to solve. First, we need to find a way to rewrite it so that there is only one variable in the equation. If we solve for x we get the equation 6x=13-1z which can be simplified to x=2z. We can then plug that into the original equation and get 6(2z)+z=13 or 13z=13 or z=1. Now we know two variables that we can use to solve for x and we can write the equation 6x+1=13 or x=2. Thus, we can tell that in hockey teams get 2 points for each regulation win (x=2) and 1 point for each overtime win (z=1).

This is a highly simplified example of algebra, but the same process works with any basic mathematical function provided you follow the order of operations. The order of operations is the order in which you have to perform each mathematical function to get the correct answer. Following the order of operations is important because while some operations can be done in any order:

(1+2)+3 = 3+3 = 6 is the same as (2+3)+1 = 5+1 = 6

others cannot:

(10-2)/4 = 8/4 = 2 is not the same as (10/4)-2 = 2.5-2 = .5

Doing the operations in any order you want can give you very incorrect results.

The order of operations goes: parentheses, exponents, multiplication, division, addition, subtraction. It can be remembered through the acronym Please Excuse My Dear Aunt Sally.

Video Tutorials - Step-by-Step Solutions

https://www.test-preparation.ca/algebra-practice-questions/

Ratios

In mathematics, a ratio is a relationship between two numbers of the same kind[1] (e.g., objects, persons, students, spoonfuls, units of whatever identical dimension), usually expressed as "a to b" or a:b, sometimes expressed arithmetically as a dimensionless quotient of the two[2] which explicitly shows how many times the first number contains the second (not necessarily an integer).[3] In layman's terms a ratio represents, simply, for every amount of one thing, how much there is of another thing. For example, suppose I have 10 pairs of socks for every pair of shoes then the ratio of shoes : socks would be 1:10 and the ratio of socks : shoes would be 10:1.

Notation and terminology

The ratio of numbers A and B can be expressed as:[4]
the ratio of A to B
A is to B
A:B

A rational number which is the quotient of A divided by B
The numbers A and B are sometimes called terms with A being the antecedent and B being the consequent.

The proportion expressing the equality of the ratios A:B and C:D is written A:B=C:D or A:B::C:D. this latter form, when spoken or written in the English language, is often expressed as
A is to B as C is to D.

Again, A, B, C, D are called the terms of the proportion. A and D are called the extremes, and B and C are called the means. The equality of three or more proportions is called a continued proportion.[5]
Ratios are sometimes used with three or more terms. The dimensions of a two by four that is ten inches long are 2:4:10.

Examples

The quantities being compared in a ratio might be physical quantities such as speed or length, or numbers of objects, or amounts of particular substances. A common example of the last case is the weight ratio of water to cement used in concrete, which is commonly stated as 1:4. This means that the weight of cement used is four times the weight of water used. It does not say anything about the total amounts of cement and water used, nor the amount of concrete being made. Equivalently it could be said that the ratio of cement to water is 4:1, that there is 4 times as much cement as water, or that there is a quarter (1/4) as much water as cement..

Older televisions have a 4:3 "aspect ratio," which means that the width is 4/3 of the height; modern wide-screen TVs have a 16:9 aspect ratio.

Fractional

If there are 2 oranges and 3 apples, the ratio of oranges to apples is 2:3, and the ratio of oranges to the total number of pieces of fruit is 2:5. These ratios can also be expressed in fraction form: there are 2/3 as many oranges as apples, and 2/5 of the pieces of fruit are oranges. If orange juice concentrate is to be diluted with water in the ratio 1:4, then one part of concentrate is mixed with four parts of water, giving five parts total; the amount of orange juice concentrate is 1/4 the amount of water, while the amount of orange juice concentrate is 1/5 of the total liquid. In both ratios and fractions, it is important to be clear what is being compared to what.

Number of terms

In general, when comparing the quantities of a two-quantity ratio, this can be expressed as a fraction derived from the ratio. For example, in a ratio of 2:3, the amount/size/volume/number of the first quantity will be that of the second quantity. This pattern also works with ratios with more than two terms. However, a ratio with more than two terms cannot be completely converted into a single fraction; a single fraction represents only one part of the ratio since a fraction can only compare two numbers. If the ratio deals with objects or amounts of objects, this is often expressed as "for every two parts of the first quantity there are three parts of the second quantity."

Percentage ratio

If we multiply all quantities involved in a ratio by the same number, the ratio remains valid. For example, a ratio of 3:2 is the same as 12:8. It is usual either to reduce terms to the lowest common denominator, or to express them in parts per hundred (percent).

If a mixture contains substances A, B, C & D in the ratio 5:9:4:2 then there are 5 parts of A for every 9 parts of B, 4 parts of C and 2 parts of D. As 5+9+4+2=20, the total mixture contains 5/20 of A (5 parts out of 20), 9/20 of B, 4/20 of C, and 2/20 of D. If we divide all numbers by the total and multiply by 100, this is converted to percentages: 25% A, 45% B, 20% C, and 10% D (equivalent to writing the ratio as 25:45:20:10).

CARTESIAN PLANE, COORDINATE PLANE AND COORDINATE GRID

To locate points and draw lines and curves, we use the coordinate plane. It also called Cartesian coordinate plane. It is a two-dimensional surface with a coordinate grid in it, which helps us to count the units. For the counting of those units, we use x-axis (horizontal scale) and y-axis (vertical scale).

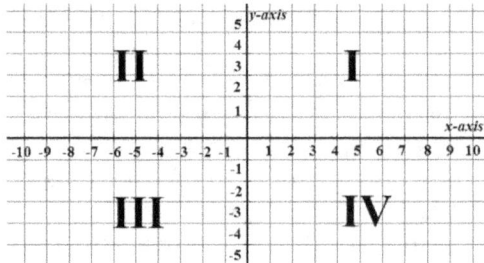

The whole system is called a coordinate system which is divided into 4 parts, called quadrants. The quadrant where all numbers are positive is the 1st quadrant (I), and if we go counterclockwise, we mark all 4 quadrants.

MATHEMATICS

The location of a dot in the coordinate system is represented by coordinates. Coordinates are represented as a pair of numbers, where the 1st number is located on the x-axis and the 2nd number is located on the y-axis. So, if a dot A has coordinates a and b, then we write:

A=(a,b)   or   A(a,b)

The point where x-axis and y-axis intersect is called an origin. The origin is the point from which we measure the distance along the x and y axes.

In the Cartesian coordinate system we can calculate the distance between 2 given points. If we have dots with coordinates:
A=(a,b)
B=(c,d)

Then the distance d between A and B can be calculated by the following formula:

$$d = \sqrt{(c-a)^2 + (d-b)^2}$$

Cartesian coordinate system is used for the drawing of 2-dimentional shapes, and is also commonly used for functions.

Example:

Draw the function   y = (1 - x)/2

To draw a linear function, we need at least 2 points.
If we put that x=0 then value for y would be:

$$y = \frac{1-x}{2} = \frac{1-0}{2} = \frac{1}{2}$$

We found the 1st point, let's name it A, with following coordinates:

A = (0,1/2)

To find the 2nd point, we can put that x=1. In this case, the value for y would be:

$$y = \frac{1-x}{2} = \frac{1-1}{2} = \frac{0}{2} = 0$$

If we denote the 2nd point with B, then the coordinates for this point are:

B=(1,0)

Since we have 2 points necessary for the function, we find them in the coordinate system and we connect them with a line that represents the function,

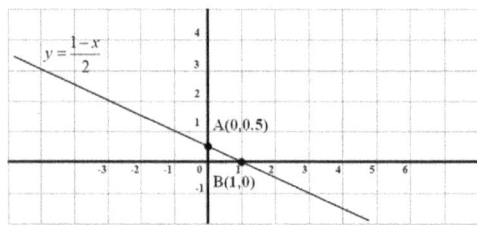

PERIMETER AREA AND VOLUME

Perimeter and Area (2-dimentional shapes)

Perimeter of a shape determines the length around that shape, while the area includes the space inside the shape.

Rectangle:

$P = 2a + 2b$
$A = ab$

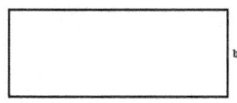

Square

$P = 4a$
$A = a^2$

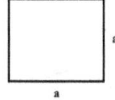

Parallelogram

$P = 2a + 2b$
$A = ah_a = bh_b$

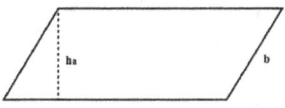

Rhombus

$P = 4a$
$A = ah = \dfrac{d_1 d_2}{2}$

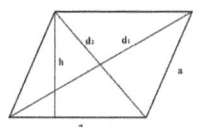

Triangle

$P = a + b + c$
$A = \dfrac{ah_a}{2} = \dfrac{bh_b}{2} = \dfrac{ch_c}{2}$

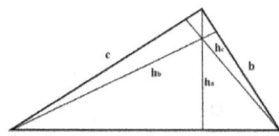

Equilateral Triangle

$P = 3a$
$A = \dfrac{a^2 \sqrt{3}}{4}$

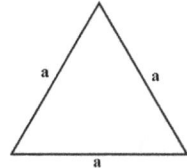

Trapezoid

$P = a+b+c+d$

$A = \dfrac{a+b}{2} h$

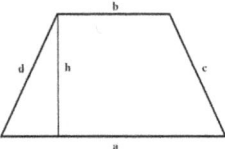

Circle

$P = 2r\pi$

$A = r^2 \pi$

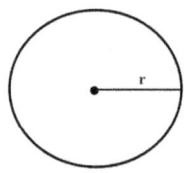

Area and Volume (3-dimentional shapes)

To calculate the area of a 3-dimentional shape, we calculate the areas of all sides and then we add them all.

To find the volume of a 3-dimentional shape, we multiply the area of the base (B) and the height (H) of the 3-dimentional shape.

$$V = BH$$

In case of a pyramid and a cone, the volume would be divided by 3.

$$V = BH/3$$

Here are some of the 3-dimentional shapes with formulas for their area and volume:

Cuboids

$A = 2(ab + bc + ac)$

$V = abc$

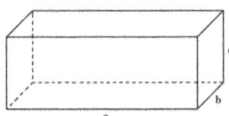

Cube

$A = 6a^2$

$V = a^3$

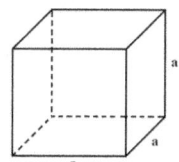

Pyramid

$A = ab + ah_a + bh_b$

$V = \dfrac{abH}{3}$

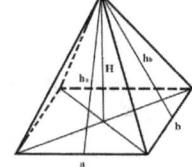

Cylinder

$A = 2r^2\pi + 2r\pi H$

$V = r^2\pi H$

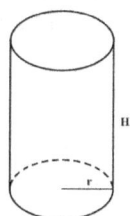

Cone

$A = (r+s)r\pi$

$V = \dfrac{r^2\pi H}{3}$

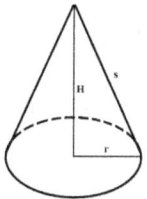

PYTHAGOREAN GEOMETRY

If we have a right triangle ABC, where its sides (legs) are a and b and c is a hypotenuse (the side opposite the right angle), then we can establish a relationship between these sides using the following formula:

$$c^2 = a^2 + b^2$$

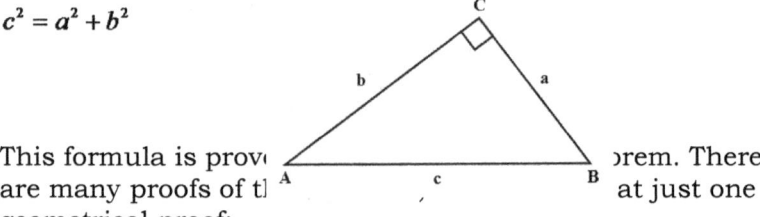

This formula is prov... ...orem. There are many proofs of t... ...at just one geometrical proof:

If we draw squares on the right triangle's sides, then the area of the square upon the hypotenuse is equal to the sum of the areas of the squares that are upon other two sides of the triangle. Since the areas of these squares are a^2, b^2 and c^2, that is how we got the formula above.

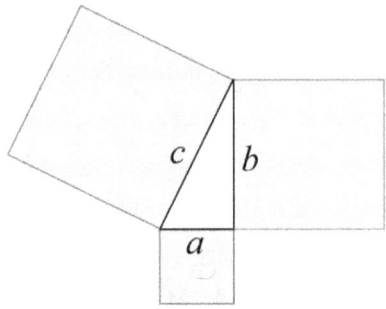

One of the famous right triangles is one with sides 3, 4 and 5. And we can see here that:

$3^2 + 4^2 = 5^2$
$9 + 16 = 25$
$25 = 25$

Example Problem:

The isosceles triangle ABC has a perimeter of 18 centimeters, and the difference between its base and legs is 3 centimeters. Find the height of this triangle.

We write the information we have about triangle ABC and we draw a picture of it for better understanding of the relation

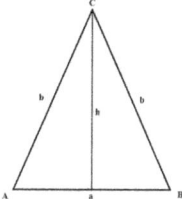

between its elements:

P=18 cm
a - b = 3 cm
h=?

We use the formula for the perimeter of the isosceles triangle, since that is what is given to us:
P = a + 2b = 18 cm

Notice that we have 2 equations with 2 variables, so we can solve it as a system of equations:

a + 2b = 18
a − b = 3 / a + 2b = 18
2a - 2b = 6 / a + 2b + 2a - 2b = 18 + 6
3a = 24
a = 24/3 = 8 cm

Now we go back to find b:
a - b = 3
8 - b = 3
b = 8 - 3
b = 5 cm

Using Pythagorean Theorem, we can find the height using a and b, because the height falls on the side a at the right angle. Notice that height cuts side a exactly in half, and that's why we use in the formula a/2. In this case, b is our hypotenuse, so we have:

$b^2 = (a/2)^2 + h^2$
$h^2 = b^2 - (a/2)^2$

$h^2 = 5^2 - (8/2)^2$
$h^2 = 5^2 - (8/2)^2$
$h^2 = 25 - 4^2$
$h^2 = 26 - 16$
$h^2 = 9$
$h = 3$ cm.

QUADRILATERALS

Quadrilaterals are 2-dimentional geometrical shapes that have 4 sides and 4 angles. There are many types of quadrilaterals, depending on the length of its sides and if they are parallel and also depending on the size of its angles. All quadrilaterals have the following properties:

Sum of all interior angles is 360^0

Sum of all exterior angles is 360^0

A quadrilateral is a parallelogram is it fulfills at least one of the following conditions:

Angles on each side are supplementary
Opposite angles are equal
Opposite sides are equal
Diagonals intersect each other exactly in half

Here are some of the quadrilaterals:

Square

All sides are equal
All angles are right angles

Rectangle

2 pairs of equal sides

All angles are right angles

Parallelogram

2 pairs of equal sides
Opposite angles are equal

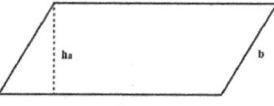

Rhombus

All sides are equal
Opposite angles are equal

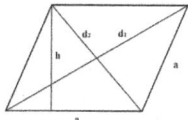

Trapezoid

One pair of parallel sides

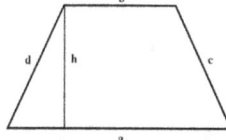

Example Problem

Find all angles of a parallelogram if one angle is greater than the other one by $40°$.

First, we draw an image of a parallelogram:

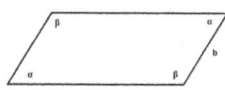

We denote angles by α and β, Since this is a parallelogram, the opposite angles are equal.

We are given that one angle is greater than the other one by $40°$, so we can write:

$β = α + 40°$

We solve this problem in two ways:

1) The sum of all internal angles of every quadrilateral is 360°. There are 2 α and 2 β. So we have:
$2α + 2β = 360°$

Now, instead of β we write α + 40:
$2α + 2(α + 40°) = 360°$
$2α + 2α + 80° = 360°$
$4α = 360° - 80°$
$4α = 280°$
$α = 280° / 4$
$α = 70°$
Now we can find β from α:
$β = α + 40°$
$β = 70° + 40°$
$β = 110°$

2) One of the conditions for parallelogram is " Angles on each side are supplementary" and we can use that to find these angles:
$α + β = 180°$
$α + α + 40° = 180°$
$2α = 180° - 40°$
$2α = 140°$
$α = 70°$

Now we find β:
$β = α + 40°$
$β = 70° + 40°$
$β = 110°$

METRIC CONVERSION - A QUICK TUTORIAL

Conversion between metric and standard units can be tricky since the units of distance, volume, area and temperature can seem arbitrary when compared to each other. Although the metric system (using SI units) is the standard system of measure in most parts of the world, many countries still use at least some of their traditional units of measure. In North

MATHEMATICS

America those units come from the old British system.

Distance

When measuring distance, the relation between metric and standard units looks like this:

0.039 in	1 millimeter	1 inch	25.4 mm
3.28 ft	1 meter	1 foot	.305 m
0.621 mi	1 kilometer	1 mile	1.61 km

Here, you can see that 1 millimeter is equal to .039 inches and 1 inch equals 25.4 millimeters.

Area

When measuring area, the relation between metric and standard looks like this:

.0016 in²	1 square millimeter	1 square inch	645.2 mm²
10.764 ft²	1 square meter	1 square foot	.093 m²
.386 mi²	1 square kilometer	1 square mile	2.59 km²
2.47 ac	hectare	1 acre	.405 ha

Volume

Similarly, when measuring volume, the relation between metric and standard units looks like this:

3034 fl oz	1 milliliter	1 fluid ounce	29.57 ml
.0264 gal	1 liter	1 gallon	3.785 L
35.314 ft³	1 cubic meter	1 cubic foot	.028 m³

Weight and Mass

When measuring weight and mass, the relation between metric and standard units looks like this:

.035 oz	1 gram	1 ounce	28.35 g
2.202 lbs	1 kilogram	1 pound	.454 kg
1.103 T	1 metric ton	1 ton	.907 t

Temperature

In predominantly metric countries the standard unit of temperature is degrees Celsius while in countries with only limited use of the metric system, such as the United States, degrees Fahrenheit is used. The chart shows the difference between Fahrenheit and Celsius:

0° Celsius	32° Fahrenheit
10° Celsius	50° Fahrenheit
20° Celsius	68° Fahrenheit
30° Celsius	86° Fahrenheit
40° Celsius	104° Fahrenheit
50° Celsius	122° Fahrenheit
60° Celsius	140° Fahrenheit
70° Celsius	158° Fahrenheit
80° Celsius	176° Fahrenheit
90° Celsius	194° Fahrenheit
100° Celsius	212° Fahrenheit

As you can see 0° C is freezing while 32° F is freezing. Similarity, 100° C is boiling compared with 212° F. To convert from Celsius to Fahrenheit you need to multiply the temperature in Celsius by 1.8, and then add 32 to it. (x° F = (y° C*1.8) + 32) To convert from Fahrenheit to Celsius you do the opposite. Subtract 32 from the temperature, then divide by 1.8. (x° C = (y° -32) / 1.8)

Mechanical Comprehension

This section contains a mechanical comprehension self-assessment and tutorials. The Tutorials are designed to familiarize general principles and the Self-Assessment contains general questions, but are not intended to be identical to the exam questions. The tutorials are *not* designed to be a complete course, and it is assumed that students have some familiarity with mechanics. If you do not understand parts of the tutorial, or find the tutorial difficult, it is recommended that you seek out additional instruction.

The questions are focused on the basic principles in Engineering and Mechanical concepts. The practice questions are designed to assess your understanding and command of basic principles. Here are the most common subject areas:

- Pulleys and Belts
- Gears
- Springs
- Levers
- Acceleration
- Basic Physics

Answer Sheet

	A	B	C	D
1	○	○	○	○
2	○	○	○	○
3	○	○	○	○
4	○	○	○	○
5	○	○	○	○
6	○	○	○	○
7	○	○	○	○
8	○	○	○	○
9	○	○	○	○
10	○	○	○	○
11	○	○	○	○
12	○	○	○	○
13	○	○	○	○
14	○	○	○	○
15	○	○	○	○
16	○	○	○	○
17	○	○	○	○
18	○	○	○	○
19	○	○	○	○
20	○	○	○	○

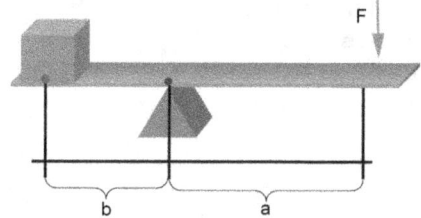

1. Consider the illustration above and the corresponding data:

Weight = W = 200 pounds
Distance from fulcrum to Weight = b = 10 feet
Distance from fulcrum to point where force is applied = a = 20 feet
How much force (F) must be applied to lift the weight?

    a. 80
    b. 100
    c. 150
    d. 200

2. A force of 20 kg. is applied to two springs in series, which compresses the springs 6 inches. If the same force is applied to springs in parallel, how far will the springs compress?

    a. 6 inches
    b. 3 inches
    c. 2 inches
    d. 1 inch

3. You are asked to determine the gear ratio of a vehicle. You open the differential and observe the ring gear the and pinion gear. The ring gear has 40 teeth and the pinion gear has 8, What is the gear ratio of the vehicle?

    a. 4:1
    b. 5:1
    c. 8:2
    d. 8:0

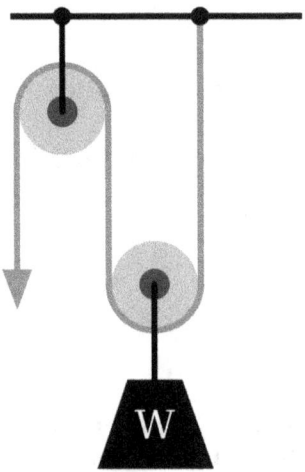

4. Consider the pulley arrangement above. If the weight, W, is 50 pounds, how much force is required to lift it?

    a. 10 pounds
    b. 20 pounds
    c. 25 pounds
    d. 50 pounds

MECHANICAL COMPREHENSION

5. Consider a gear train with 3 gears, from left to right, A with 20 teeth, gear B with 60 teeth, and gear C with 10 teeth. Gear A turns clockwise at 60 rpm. What direction and speed in rpm does Gear C turn?

    a. 120 rpm, clockwise

    b. 100 rpm clockwise

    c. 120 rpm counter clockwise

    d. 140 rpm counter clockwise

6. If a 100-pound object is sitting on a 10-square-inch plate, what is the PSI?

    a. 5

    b. 10

    c. 15

    d. 20

7. What is mechanical advantage?

    a. The ratio of energy input to energy output, typically where the input is less than the output.

    b. The ratio of energy input to energy output, typically where the input is greater than the output.

    c. The ratio of energy resistance to energy output, typically where the resistance is less than the output.

    d. None of the above

8. What is the ratio of mechanical advantage of a simple pulley?

    a. 2:1

    b. 1:1

    c. 3:1

    d. 1:2

9. Consider moving an object with a lever and a fulcrum. What is the relationship between the distance from the fulcrum and the speed the object will move?

   a. The farther away from the fulcrum, the faster the object will move.

   b. The closer to the fulcrum, the faster an object will move.

   c. An object will move the fastest when directly above the fulcrum.

   d. None of the above.

10. Which of the following are examples of a wedge?

   a. Corkscrew
   b. Scissors
   c. Wheelbarrow
   d. Pulley

11. Which of the following illustrates the principal of the lever?

   a. The greater the distance over which the force is applied, the greater the force required (to lift the load).

   b. The greater the distance over which the force is applied, the smaller the force required (to lift the load).

   c. The smaller the distance over which the force is applied, the smaller the force required (to lift the load).

   d. None of the above

12. Consider two gears on separate shafts that mesh. The input gear has 30 teeth and turns at 100 rpm. If the output gear has 40 teeth, how fast is the output gear turning?

   a. 300 rpm
   b. 250 rpm
   c. 75 rpm

d. 100 rpm

13. Consider two gears on separate shafts that mesh. The input gear has 100 teeth and turns at 50 rpm. If the output gear has 20 teeth, how fast is the output gear turning?

    a. 300 rpm
    b. 250 rpm
    c. 200 rpm
    d. 100 rpm

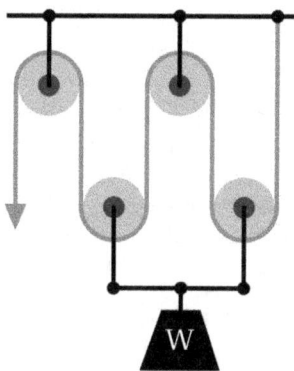

14. Consider the pulley arrangement above. If the weight is 100 pounds, how much force is required to lift it?

    a. 20 pounds
    b. 33 pounds
    c. 50 pounds
    d. 75 pounds

15. Tension of 40 kg. is applied to two springs in parallel, which expands the springs 8 inches. If the same force is applied to springs in series, how far will the springs expand?

   a. 2 inches
   b. 4 inches
   c. 8 inches
   d. 16 inches

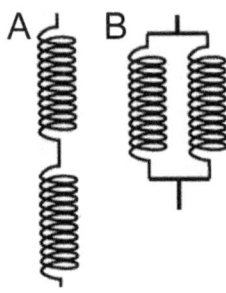

16. Consider the diagram above and select the correct labels from the options below.

   a. A - series, B - parallel
   b. A - parallel, B - series
   c. Series and parallel do not apply to springs
   d. None of the above

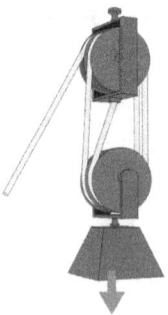

17. Consider the pulley arrangement above. If the weight is 200 pounds, how much force must be exerted downward on the rope?

    a. 200 pounds
    b. 100 pounds
    c. 50 pounds
    d. 25 pounds

18. Up-and-down or back-and-forth motion is called:

    a. Rotary motion
    b. Reciprocating motion
    c. Agitation motion
    d. Harmonic motion

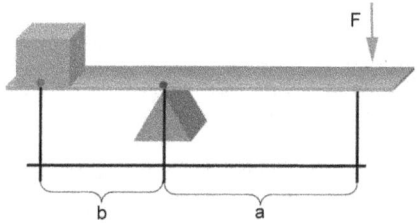

19. Consider the illustration above and the corresponding data:
Weight = W = 80 pounds
Distance from fulcrum to Weight = b = 10 feet
Distance from fulcrum to point where force is applied = a = 20 feet
How much force (F) must be applied to lift the weight?

    a. 80
    b. 40
    c. 20
    d. 10

20. The output torque of a 2 gear train is 1,000 newton-meters, and the gear ratio is 2:1. What is the input force?

    a. 200
    b. 400
    c. 500
    d. 1000

Mechanical Comprehension

Answer Key

1. B
To solve for F, Weight X b (distance from fulcrum to weight) = Force X a (distance from fulcrum to point where force is applied)
200 X 10 = F X 20
2000/20 = F
F = 100

2. B
If the springs in series compress 6 inches, then the springs in parallel will compress half that amount, or 3 inches.

3. B
Opening the differential, the ring gear is the larger gear and the pinion the smaller. The gear differential is calculated by dividing the number of teeth on the pinion into the number of teeth on the ring gear. 40/8 = 5, or 5:1.

4. C
Since the weight is only attached to one pulley, the force required will be 50/2 = 25 pounds.

5. A
First calculate the speed of gear B. The gear ratio is 60:20 or 3:1. If gear A is turning at 60 rpm, then gear B will turn at 30/3 = 20 rpm.

Next calculate B and C. Gear C is smaller, so it will turn faster. The gear ratio is 60:10 or 6:1, and since gear B turns at 20 rpm, gear C will turn at 20 X 6 = 120 rpm.

Next calculate the direction. Gear A is turning clockwise, so Gear B is turning counter-clockwise, so gear C must be turning clockwise.

6. B
Calculate the PSI by taking the weight divided by the size of the object the weight is bearing on. 100/10 = 10 PSI.

7. A
Mechanical advantage is the ratio of energy input to energy output, typically where the input is less than the output. Mechanical advantage is a measure of the force amplification achieved by using a tool, mechanical device or machine system. Ideally, the device preserves the input power and simply trades off forces against movement to obtain a desired amplification in the output force. The model for this is the law of the lever. Machine components designed to manage forces and movement in this way are called mechanisms.

8. B
The ratio of mechanical advantage of a simple pulley is 1:1.

9. A
The farther away from the fulcrum, the faster the object will move.

10. B
Examples of wedges include the cutting edge of scissors, knives, screwdrivers, doorstops, nails axes and chisels.

11. B
The greater the distance over which the force is applied, the smaller the force required (to lift the load).

12. C
Call the input gear G^1 and the output gear G^2. Call the speed of G^1, S^1 and the number of teeth T^1. Similarly for G^2, we have S^2 and T^2.
Given data:
$S^1 = 100$
$T^1 = 30$
$S^2 = $ unknown
$T^2 = 40$
We know that $S^1 \times T^1 = S^2 \times T^2$
So, $100 \times 30 = S^2 \times 40$
$S^2 = 3000/40 = 75$ rpm

13. B
Call the input gear G^1 and the output gear G^2. Call the speed of G^1, S^1 and the number of teeth T^1. Similarly for G^2, we have S^2 and T^2.

MECHANICAL COMPREHENSION

Given data
$S^1 - 50$
$T^1 = 100$
$S^2 = $ unknown
$T^2 = 20$
We know that $S^1 \times T^1 = S^2 \times T^2$

So, $50 \times 100 = S^2 \times 20$
$S^2 = 5000/20 = 250$ rpm

14. B
Notice the weight is attached to one end of the rope and to one pulley. The force required to lift a 100 pound weight with this arrangement is 100/3 = 33.

15. A
If the springs in parallel expand 10 inches, then the springs in series will expand twice that amount, or 20 inches.

16. A
The correct labels are, A - series, B - parallel

17. C
50 pounds of force much be exerted downward on the rope to lift the 200 pound weight. Since there are 4 pulleys, each will take 1/4 of the load. 200/4 = 50 pounds.

18. B
Up-and-down or back-and-forth motion is called reciprocal motion.

19. B
To solve for F, Weight X b (distance from fulcrum to weight) = Force X a (distance from fulcrum to point where force is applied)
$80 \times 10 = F \times 20$
$800/20 = F$
$F = 40$

20. C
If the output force is 1,000 newton-meters, and the gear ration is 2:1, the input force will be 1,000/2 = 500.

Overview of Simple Machines

1. Lever

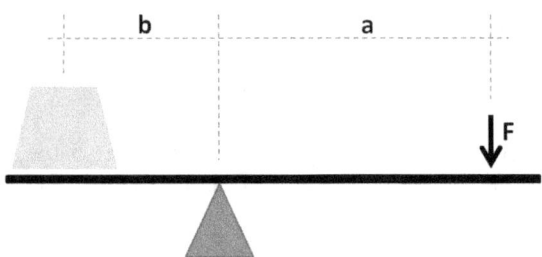

The lever is a movable bar that pivots on a fulcrum attached to a fixed point. The lever operates by applying forces at different distances from the fulcrum, or pivot.

Assuming the lever does not dissipate or store energy, the power into the lever must equal the power out of the lever. As the lever rotates around the fulcrum, points farther from this pivot move faster than points closer to the pivot. Therefore a force applied to a point farther from the pivot must be less than the force located at a point closer in, because power is the product of force and velocity.

This is the law of the lever, which was proven by Archimedes using geometric reasoning. It shows that if the distance a from the fulcrum to where the input force is applied (point A) is greater than the distance b from fulcrum to where the output force is applied (point B), then the lever amplifies the input force. On the other hand, if the distance a from the fulcrum to the input force is less than the distance b from the fulcrum to the output force, then the lever reduces the input force.

Here is a sample question:

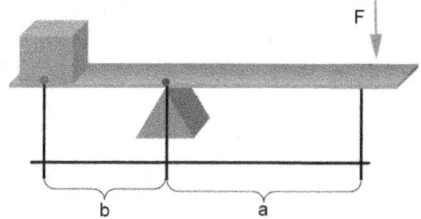

Consider the illustration above and the corresponding data:

Weight = W = 100 pounds
Distance from fulcrum to Weight = b = 2 feet
Distance from fulcrum to point where force is applied = a = 5 feet
How much force (F) must be applied to lift the weight?

a. 100
b. 40
c. 25
d. 10

Answer: B

Solution:

We know that the lever does not store energy, so the to solve for F, Weight X b (distance from fulcrum to weight) = Force X a (distance from fulcrum to point where force is applied)
100 X 2 = F X 5
200/5 = F
F = 40

2. PULLEYS

A pulley is a wheel on an axle that is designed to support movement of a cable or belt along its circumference. Pulleys are used in a variety of ways to lift loads, apply forces, and to transmit power.

A pulley is also called a sheave or drum and may have a groove between two flanges around its circumference. The drive element of a pulley system can be a rope, cable, belt, or chain that runs over the pulley inside the groove.

A rope and pulley system, that is a block and tackle, is characterized by the use of a single continuous rope to transmit a tension force around one or more pulleys to lift or move a load—the rope may be a light line or a strong cable.

If the rope and pulley system does not dissipate or store energy, then its mechanical advantage is the number of parts of the rope that act on the load. This can be shown as follows.

Consider the set of pulleys that form the moving block and the parts of the rope that support this block. If there are p of these parts of the rope supporting the load W, then a force balance on the moving block shows that the tension in each of the parts of the rope must be W/p. This means the input force on the rope is T=W/p. Thus, the block and tackle reduces the input force by the factor p.

3. Wedge

A wedge is a triangular shaped round tool, a compound and portable inclined plane, and one of the six classical simple machines. It can be used to separate two objects or portions of an object, lift an object, or hold an object in place. It functions by converting a force applied to its blunt end into forces perpendicular (normal) to its inclined surfaces. The mechanical advantage of a wedge is given by the ratio of the length of its slope to its width. Although a short wedge with a wide angle may do a job faster, it requires more force than a long wedge with a narrow angle.

4. Screw

A screw is a mechanism that converts rotational motion to linear motion, and a torque (rotational force) to a linear force. It is one of the six classical simple machines. The most common form consists of a cylindrical shaft with heli-

Mechanical Comprehension

cal grooves or ridges called threads around the outside. The screw passes through a hole in another object or medium, with threads on the inside of the hole that mesh with the screw's threads.

A screw can amplify force; a small rotational force (torque) on the shaft can exert a large axial force on a load. The smaller the pitch, the distance between the screw's threads, the greater the mechanical advantage, the ratio of output to input force. Screws are widely used in threaded fasteners to hold objects together, and in devices such as screw tops for containers, vises, screw jacks and screw presses.

5. Gears and Gear Trains

A gear train is formed by mounting gears on a frame so that the teeth of the gears engage. Gear teeth are designed to ensure the pitch circles of engaging gears roll on each other without slipping, this provides a smooth transmission of rotation from one gear to the next.

Here is a sample question:

Consider 3 meshed gears. Gear A has 20 teeth, Gear B has 60 teeth and Gear C has 10 teeth. Gear A revolves clockwise at 60 rpm. How fast does gear C turn and in what direction?

First, figure out the direction because that is easier. Gear A turn clockwise, which will turn gear B counter-clockwise. Now gear C, meshed with gear B will turn clockwise.

To calculate the speed of gear C, first calculate the speed of gear B.

To calculate the speed of gear B, first calculate the gear ration by,
No. of teeth of gear B / No. of teeth of gear A

60/20 = 3 (or gear ratio of 1:3 : Gear B : Gear A)

So gear B will turn 3 times for every complete turn of gear A.

To calculate the speed of gear B, divide, 60/3 = 20 rpm.

This makes sense since gear B is three times the size of gear A (60 teeth to gear A's 20) so it turns much slower.

To calculate the speed of gear C, calculate the gear ration and then divide by the speed of gear B.

Notice that gear C is quite a bit smaller (10 teeth to gear B's 60 teeth), so we expect gear C will turn much faster.

First calculate the gear ratio: 60/10 = 6, or 6:1 : Gear C : Gear B.

Gear B is turning at 20 rpm - multiplying the speed is, 20 rpm X 6 = 120.

Gear C is turning at 120 rpm.

Practice Test
Questions Set 1

The questions below are not the same as you will find on the Ironworkers Test - that would be too easy! And nobody knows what the questions will be and they change all the time. Below are general questions that cover the same subject areas as the Ironworkers Test. So, while the format and exact wording of the questions may differ slightly, and change from year to year, if you can answer the questions below, you will have no problem with the Ironworkers Test.

For the best results, take these Practice Test Questions as if it were the real exam. Set aside time when you will not be disturbed, and a location that is quiet and free of distractions. Read the instructions carefully, read each question carefully, and answer to the best of your ability.
Use the bubble answer sheets provided. When you have completed the Practice Questions, check your answer against the Answer Key and read the explanation provided.

Do not attempt more than one set of practice test questions in one day. After completing the first practice test, wait two or three days before attempting the second set of questions.

Reading Comprehension

	A	B	C	D	E		A	B	C	D	E
1	○	○	○	○	○	21	○	○	○	○	○
2	○	○	○	○	○	22	○	○	○	○	○
3	○	○	○	○	○	23	○	○	○	○	○
4	○	○	○	○	○	24	○	○	○	○	○
5	○	○	○	○	○	25	○	○	○	○	○
6	○	○	○	○	○	26	○	○	○	○	○
7	○	○	○	○	○	27	○	○	○	○	○
8	○	○	○	○	○	28	○	○	○	○	○
9	○	○	○	○	○	29	○	○	○	○	○
10	○	○	○	○	○	30	○	○	○	○	○
11	○	○	○	○	○						
12	○	○	○	○	○						
13	○	○	○	○	○						
14	○	○	○	○	○						
15	○	○	○	○	○						
16	○	○	○	○	○						
17	○	○	○	○	○						
18	○	○	○	○	○						
19	○	○	○	○	○						
20	○	○	○	○	○						

Basic Math and Problem Solving

	A	B	C	D	E		A	B	C	D	E
1	○	○	○	○	○	31	○	○	○	○	○
2	○	○	○	○	○	32	○	○	○	○	○
3	○	○	○	○	○	33	○	○	○	○	○
4	○	○	○	○	○	34	○	○	○	○	○
5	○	○	○	○	○	35	○	○	○	○	○
6	○	○	○	○	○	36	○	○	○	○	○
7	○	○	○	○	○	37	○	○	○	○	○
8	○	○	○	○	○	38	○	○	○	○	○
9	○	○	○	○	○	39	○	○	○	○	○
10	○	○	○	○	○	40	○	○	○	○	○
11	○	○	○	○	○	41	○	○	○	○	○
12	○	○	○	○	○	42	○	○	○	○	○
13	○	○	○	○	○	43	○	○	○	○	○
14	○	○	○	○	○	44	○	○	○	○	○
15	○	○	○	○	○	45	○	○	○	○	○
16	○	○	○	○	○	46	○	○	○	○	○
17	○	○	○	○	○	47	○	○	○	○	○
18	○	○	○	○	○	48	○	○	○	○	○
19	○	○	○	○	○	49	○	○	○	○	○
20	○	○	○	○	○	50	○	○	○	○	○
21	○	○	○	○	○	51	○	○	○	○	○
22	○	○	○	○	○	52	○	○	○	○	○
23	○	○	○	○	○	53	○	○	○	○	○
24	○	○	○	○	○	54	○	○	○	○	○
25	○	○	○	○	○	55	○	○	○	○	○
26	○	○	○	○	○	56	○	○	○	○	○
27	○	○	○	○	○	57	○	○	○	○	○
28	○	○	○	○	○	58	○	○	○	○	○
29	○	○	○	○	○	59	○	○	○	○	○
30	○	○	○	○	○	60	○	○	○	○	○

Mechanical Comprehension

	A	B	C	D
1	○	○	○	○
2	○	○	○	○
3	○	○	○	○
4	○	○	○	○
5	○	○	○	○
6	○	○	○	○
7	○	○	○	○
8	○	○	○	○
9	○	○	○	○
10	○	○	○	○
11	○	○	○	○
12	○	○	○	○
13	○	○	○	○
14	○	○	○	○
15	○	○	○	○
16	○	○	○	○
17	○	○	○	○
18	○	○	○	○
19	○	○	○	○
20	○	○	○	○

Practice Test Questions 1

Reading Comprehension

Directions: The following questions are based on several reading passages. A series of questions follow each passage. Read each passage carefully, and then answer the questions based on it. You may reread the passage as often as you wish. When you have finished answering the questions based on one passage, go right onto the next passage. Choose the best answer based on the information given and implied.

Questions 1 – 4 refer to the following passage.

Passage 1 - The Life of Helen Keller

Many people have heard of Helen Keller. She is famous because she was unable to see or hear, but learned to speak and read and went onto attend college and earn a degree. Her life is a very interesting story, one that she developed into an autobiography, which was then adapted into both a stage play and a movie. How did Helen Keller overcome her disabilities to become a famous woman? Read on to find out. Helen Keller was not born blind and deaf. When she was a small baby, she had a very high fever for several days. As a result of her sudden illness, baby Helen lost her eyesight and her hearing. Because she was so young when she went deaf and blind, Helen Keller never had any recollection of being able to see or hear. Since she could not hear, she could not learn to talk. Since she could not see, it was difficult for her to move around. For the first six years of her life, her world was very still and dark.

Imagine what Helen's childhood was like. She could not hear her mother's voice. She could not see the beauty of her parent's farm. She could not recognize who was giving her a hug, or a bath or even where her bedroom was each night. Worse, she could not communicate with her parents in any way. She could not express her feelings or tell them the things she wanted. It must have been a very sad childhood. When Helen was six years old, her parents hired her a teacher named Anne Sullivan. Anne was a young woman who was almost blind. However, she could hear and she could read Braille, so she was a perfect teacher for young Helen. At first, Anne had a very hard time teaching Helen anything. She described her first impression of Helen as a "wild thing, not a child." Helen did not like Anne at first either. She bit and hit Anne when Anne tried to teach her. However, the two of them eventually came to have a great deal of love and respect.

Anne taught Helen to hear by putting her hands on people's throats. She could feel the sounds people made. In time, Helen learned to feel what people said. Next, Anne taught Helen to read Braille, which is a way that books are written for the blind. Finally, Anne taught Helen to talk. Although Helen did learn to talk, it was hard for anyone but Anne to understand her.

As Helen grew older, she amazed more and more people with her story. She went to college and wrote books about her life. She gave talks to the public, with Anne at her side, translating her words. Today, both Anne Sullivan and Helen Keller are famous women who are respected for their lives' work.

1. Helen Keller could not see and hear and so, what was her biggest problem in childhood?

    a. Inability to communicate

    b. Inability to walk

    c. Inability to play

    d. Inability to eat

2. Helen learned to hear by feeling the vibrations people made when they spoke. What were these vibrations were felt through?

    a. Mouth

    b. Throat

    c. Ears

    d. Lips

3. From the passage, we can infer that Anne Sullivan was a patient teacher. We can infer this because

    a. Helen hit and bit her and Anne remained her teacher.

    b. Anne taught Helen to read only.

    c. Anne was hard of hearing too.

    d. Anne wanted to be a teacher.

4. Helen Keller learned to speak but Anne translated her words when she spoke in public. The reason Helen needed a translator was because

    a. Helen spoke another language.

    b. Helen's words were hard for people to understand.

    c. Helen spoke very quietly.

    d. Helen did not speak but only used sign language.

Questions 5 – 7 refer to the following passage.

Passage 2 - Ways Characters Communicate in Theater

Playwrights give their characters voices in a way that gives depth and added meaning to what happens on stage during their play. There are different types of speech in scripts that allow characters to talk with themselves, with other characters, and even with the audience.

It is very unique to theater that characters may talk "to themselves." When characters do this, the speech they give is called a soliloquy. Soliloquies are usually poetic, introspective, moving, and can tell audience members about the feelings, motivations, or suspicions of an individual character without that character having to reveal them to other characters on stage. "To be or not to be" is a famous soliloquy given by Hamlet as he considers difficult but important themes, such as life and death.

The most common type of communication in plays is when one character is speaking to another or a group of other characters. This is generally called dialogue, but can also be called monologue if one character speaks without being interrupted for a long time. It is not necessarily the most important type of communication, but it is the most common because the plot of the play cannot really progress without it.

Lastly, and most unique to theater (although it has been used somewhat in film) is when a character speaks directly to the audience. This is called an aside, and scripts usually specifically direct actors to do this. Asides are usually comical, an inside joke between the character and the audience, and very short. The actor will usually face the audience when delivering them, even if it's for a moment, so the audience can recognize this move as an aside.

All three of these types of communication are important to the art of theater, and have been perfected by famous playwrights like Shakespeare. Understanding these types of communication can help an audience member grasp what is artful about the script and action of a play.

5. According to the passage, characters in plays communicate to

    a. move the plot forward

    b. show the private thoughts and feelings of one character

    c. make the audience laugh

    d. add beauty and artistry to the play

6. When Hamlet delivers "To be or not to be," he can most likely be described as

    a. solitary

    b. thoughtful

    c. dramatic

    d. hopeless

7. The author uses parentheses to punctuate "although it has been used somewhat in film,"

    a. to show that films are less important

    b. instead of using commas so that the sentence is not interrupted

    c. because parenthesis help separate details that are not as important

    d. to show that films are not as artistic

Questions 8 – 11 refer to the following passage.

Passage 3 - Low Blood Sugar

As the name suggest, low blood sugar is low sugar levels in the bloodstream. This can occur when you have not eaten properly and undertake strenuous activity, or, when you are very hungry. When Low blood sugar occurs regularly and is ongoing, it is a medical condition called hypoglycaemia. This condition can occur in diabetics and in healthy adults.

Causes of low blood sugar can include excessive alcohol consumption, metabolic problems, stomach surgery, pancreas, liver or kidneys problems, as well as a side-effect of some medications.

Symptoms

There are different symptoms depending on the severity of the case.

Mild hypoglycaemia can lead to feelings of nausea and hunger. The patient may also feel nervous, jittery and have fast heart beats. Sweaty skin, clammy and cold skin are likely symptoms.
Moderate hypoglycaemia can result in a short temper, confusion, nervousness, fear and blurring of vision. The patient may feel weak and unsteady.

Severe cases of hypoglycaemia can lead to seizures, coma, fainting spells, nightmares, headaches, excessive sweats and severe tiredness.

Diagnosis of low blood sugar

A doctor can diagnosis this medical condition by asking the patient questions and testing blood and urine samples. Home testing kits are available for patients to monitor blood sugar levels. It is important to see a qualified doctor though. The doctor can administer tests to safely rule out other medical conditions that could affect blood sugar levels.

Treatment

Quick treatments include drinking or eating foods and drinks with high sugar contents. Good examples include soda, fruit juice, hard candy and raisins. Glucose energy tablets can also help. Doctors may also recommend medications and well as changes in diet and exercise routine to treat chronic low blood sugar.

8. Based on the article, which of the following is true?

    a. Low blood sugar can happen to anyone.

    b. Low blood sugar only happens to diabetics.

    c. Low blood sugar can occur even.

    d. None of the statements are true.

9. Which of the following are the author's opinion?

    a. Quick treatments include drinking or eating foods and drinks with high sugar contents.

    b. None of the statements are opinions.

    c. This condition can occur in diabetics and also in healthy adults.

    d. There are different symptoms depending on the severity of the case

10. What is the author's purpose?

    a. To inform

    b. To persuade

    c. To entertain

    d. To analyse

11. Which of the following is not a detail?

    a. A doctor can diagnosis this medical condition by asking the patient questions and testing.

    b. A doctor will test blood and urine samples.

    c. Glucose energy tablets can also help.

    d. Home test kits monitor blood sugar levels.

    d. None of the above.

Questions 12 – 15 refer to the following passage.

How To Get A Good Nights Sleep

Sleep is just as essential for healthy living as water, air and food. Sleep allows the body to rest and replenish depleted energy levels. Sometimes we may, for various reasons, have trouble sleeping which has a serious effect on our health. Those who have prolonged sleeping problems are facing a serious medical condition and should see a qualified doctor when possible for help. Here is simple guide that can help you sleep better at night.

Try to create a natural pattern of waking up and sleeping around the same time every day. This means avoiding going to bed too early and oversleeping past your usual wake up time. Going to bed and getting up at radically different times everyday confuses your body clock. Try to establish a natural rhythm as much as you can.

Exercises and a bit of physical activity can help you sleep better at night. If you are having problem sleeping, try to be as active as you can during the day. If you are tired from physical activity, falling asleep is a natural and easy process for your body. If you remain inactive during the day, you will find it harder to sleep properly at night. Try walking, jogging, swimming or simple stretches as you get close to your bed time.

Afternoon naps are great to refresh you during the day, but they may also keep you awake at night. If you feel sleepy during the day, get up, take a walk and get busy to keep from sleeping. Stretching is a good way to increase blood flow to the brain and keep you alert so that you don't sleep during the day. This will help you sleep better night.

> A warm bath or a glass of milk in the evening can help your body relax and prepare for sleep. A cold bath will wake you up and keep you up for several hours. Also avoid eating too late before bed.

12. How would you describe this sentence?

    a. A recommendation

    b. An opinion

    c. A fact

    d. A diagnosis

13. Which of the following is an alternative title for this article?

    a. Exercise and a good night's sleep

    b. Benefits of a good night's sleep

    c. Tips for a good night's sleep

    d. Lack of sleep is a serious medical condition

14. Which of the following cannot be inferred from this article?

    a. Biking is helpful for getting a good night's sleep

    b. Mental activity is helpful for getting a good night's sleep

    c. Eating bedtime snacks is not recommended

    d. Getting up at the same time is helpful for a good night's sleep

15. What is a disadvantage of taking naps?

    a. They may keep you awake.

    b. There are no disadvantages

    c. They may help you sleep better

    d. They may affect your diet

Question 16 refers to the following Table of Contents.

Contents

    Science Self-assessment 81
    Answer Key 91
    Science Tutorials 96
    Scientific Method 96
    Biology 99
    Heredity: Genes and Mutation 104
    Classification 108
    Ecology 110
    Chemistry 112
    Energy: Kinetic and Mechanical 126
    Energy: Work and Power 130
    Force: Newton's Three Laws 132

16. Consider the table of contents above. What page would you find information about natural selection and adaptation?

    a. 81
    b. 90
    c. 110
    d. 132

Questions 17 – 20 refer to the following passage.

Passage 5 - Pearl Harbor

A Day That Will Live in Infamy! Attack on Pearl Harbor
In 1941, the world was at war. The United States was trying very hard to keep itself out of the conflict. In Europe, the countries of Germany and Italy had formed an alliance to expand their land and territory. Germany had already taken over Poland, Denmark, and parts of France. They were heading next toward England and due to all the fighting in Europe, there were battles taking place as far south as North Africa, where the German and Italian armies were fighting the British.

This got even worse when the Asian nation of Japan formed an alliance with Germany and Italy. Together, the three countries called themselves, the AXIS. Now, the war was in the Pacific as well as in Europe and Northern Africa. A great deal of Americans felt that perhaps now was the time for the United States to join with its ally, Great Britain and stop the Axis from taking over more regions of the world.

In 1941, Franklin Roosevelt was President of the United States. His fear at the time was that Japan would try to take over many countries in Asia. He did not want to see that happen, so he moved some of the United States warships that had been stationed in San Diego, to the military base at Pearl Harbor, in Honolulu, Hawaii.

Japan quietly plotted their attack. They waited until the early hours of the morning on Sunday, December 7, 1941. Then, 350 Japanese war plans began to drop bombs on the U.S. ships at Pearl Harbor. The first bombs fell at 7:48 am and a mere 90 minutes later, the attack was over. Pearl Harbor was decimated. 8 battleships were damaged. Eleven ships were sunk and 300 U.S. planes were destroyed. Most devastating was the loss of life 2,400 U.S. military members was killed in the attack and 1, 282 were injured.

President Roosevelt addressed the country via the radio and said "Today is a day that will live in infamy." He asked Congress to declare war on Japan. War was declared on Japan on December 8th and on Germany and Italy on December 11th. The United States had entered World War Two.

17. After reading the passage, what can we infer infamy means?

    a. Famous

    b. Remembered in a good way

    c. Remembered in a bad way

    d. Easily forgotten

18. What three countries formed the Axis?

    a. Italy, England, Germany

    b. United States, England, Italy

    c. Germany, Japan, Italy

    d. Germany, Japan, United States

19. What do you think was President Roosevelt's reason for moving warships to Pearl Harbor?

    a. He feared Japan would bomb San Diego

    b. He knew Japan was going to attack Pearl Harbor

    c. He was planning to attack Japan

    d. He wanted to try and protect Asian countries from Japanese takeover

20. Why do you think Japan chose a Sunday morning at 7:48 am for their attack?

    a. They knew the military slept late

    b. There is a law against bombing countries on a Sunday

    c. They wanted the attack to catch people by surprise

    d. That was the only free time they had to attack.

Questions 21 - 24 refer to the following recipe.

If You Have Allergies, You're Not Alone

People who experience allergies might joke that their immune systems have let them down or are seriously lacking. Truthfully though, people who experience allergic reactions or allergy symptoms during certain times of the year have heightened immune systems that are, "better" than those of people who have perfectly healthy but less militant immune systems.

Still, when a person has an allergic reaction, they are having an adverse reaction to a substance that is considered normal to most people. Mild allergic reactions usually have symptoms like itching, runny nose, red eyes, or bumps or discoloration of the skin. More serious allergic reactions, such as those to animal and insect poisons or certain foods, may result in the closing of the throat, swelling of the eyes, low blood pressure, inability to breath, and can even be fatal.

Different treatments help different allergies, and which one a person uses depends on the nature and severity of the allergy. It is recommended to patients with severe allergies to take extra precautions, such as carrying an EpiPen, which treats anaphylactic shock and may prevent death, always in order for the remedy to be readily available and more effective. When an allergy is not so severe, treatments may be used just relieve a person of uncomfortable symptoms. Over the counter allergy medicines treat milder symptoms, and can be bought at any grocery store and used in moderation to help people with allergies live normally.

There are many tests available to assess whether a person has allergies or what they may be allergic to, and advances in these tests and the medicine used to treat patients continues to improve. Despite this fact, allergies still affect many people throughout the year or even every day. Medicines used to treat allergies have side effects of their own, and it is difficult to bring the body into balance with the use of medicine. Regardless, many of those who live with allergies are grateful for what is available and find it useful in maintaining their lifestyles.

21. According to this passage, the word that the word "militant" belongs in a group with the words:

    a. sickly, ailing, faint

    b. strength, power, vigor

    c. active, fighting, warring

    d. worn, tired, breaking down

22. The author says that "medicines used to treat allergies have side-effects of their own" to

    a. point out that doctors aren't very good at diagnosing and treating allergies

    b. argue that because of the large number of people with allergies, a cure will never be found

    c. explain that allergy medicines aren't cures and some compromise must be made

    d. argue that more wholesome remedies should be researched and medicines banned

23. It can be inferred that _____ recommend that some people with allergies carry medicine with them.

    a. the author

    b. doctors

    c. the makers of EpiPen

    d. people with allergies

24. The author has written this passage to

    a. inform readers on symptoms of allergies so people with allergies can get help

    b. persuade readers to be proud of having allergies

    c. inform readers on different remedies so people with allergies receive the right help

    d. describe different types of allergies, their symptoms, and their remedies

Questions 25 – 26 refer to the following email.

SUBJECT: MEDICAL STAFF CHANGES

To all staff:

This email is to advise you of a paper on recommended medical staff changes has been posted to the Human Resources website.

The contents are of primary interest to medical staff, other staff may be interested in reading it, particularly those in medical support roles.

The paper deals with several major issues:

    1. Improving our ability to attract top quality staff to the hospital, and retain our existing staff. These changes will make our position and departmental names internationally recognizable and comparable with North American and North Asian departments and positions.

    2. Improving our ability to attract top quality staff by introducing greater flexibility in the departmental structure.

    3. General comments on issues to be further discussed in relation to research staff.

The changes outlined in this paper are significant. I encourage you to read the document and send to me any comments you may have, so that it can be enhanced and improved.

Gordon Simms
Administrator,
Seven Oaks Regional Hospital

25. Are all hospital staff required to read the document posted to the Human Resources website?

    a. Yes all staff are required to read the document.

    b. No, reading the document is optional.

    c. Only medical staff are required to read the document.

    d. none of the above are correct.

26. Have the changes to medical staff been made?

    a. Yes, the changes have been made.

    b. No, the changes are only being discussed.

    c. Some of the changes have been made.

    d. None of the choices are correct.

Questions 27 – 30 refer to the following passage.

When a Poet Longs to Mourn, He Writes an Elegy

Poems are an expressive, especially emotional, form of writing. They have been present in literature virtually from the time civilizations invented the written word. Poets often portrayed as moody, secluded, and even troubled, but this is because poets are introspective and feel deeply about the current events and cultural norms they are surrounded with. Poets often produce the most telling literature, giving insight into the society and mind-set they come from. This can be done in many forms.

The oldest types of poems often include many stanzas, may or may not rhyme, and are more about telling a story than experimenting with language or words. The most common types of ancient poetry are epics, which are usually extremely long stories that follow a hero through his journey, or ellegies, which are often solemn in tone and used to mourn or lament something or someone. The Mesopotamians are often said to have invented the written word, and their literature is among the oldest in the world, including the epic poem titled "Epic of Gilgamesh." Similar in style and length to "Gilgamesh" is "Beowulf," an ellegy written in Old English and set in Scandinavia. These poems are often used by professors as the earliest examples of literature.

The importance of poetry was revived in the Renaissance. At this time, Europeans discovered the style and beauty of ancient Greek arts, and poetry was among those. Shakespeare is the most well-known poet of the time, and he used poetry not only to write poems but also to write plays for the theater. The most popular forms of poetry during the Renaissance included villanelles, (a nineteen-line poetic form) sonnets, as well as the epic. Poets during this time focused on style and form, and developed very specific rules and outlines for how an exceptional poem should be written.

As often happens in the arts, modern poets have rejected the constricting rules of Renaissance poets, and free form poems are much more popular. Some modern poems would read just like stories if they weren't arranged into lines and stanzas. It is difficult to tell which poems and poets will be the most important, because works of art often become more famous in hindsight, after the poet has died and society can look at itself without being in the moment. Modern poetry continues to develop, and will no doubt continue to change as values, thought, and writing continue to change.

Poems can be among the most enlightening and uplifting texts for a person to read if they are looking to connect with the past, connect with other people, or try to gain an understanding of what is happening in their time.

PRACTICE TEST QUESTIONS 1

27. In summary, the author has written this passage

    a. as a foreword that will introduce a poem in a book or magazine

    b. because she loves poetry and wants more people to like it

    c. to give a brief history of poems

    d. to convince students to write poems

28. The author organizes the paragraphs mainly by

    a. moving chronologically, explaining which types of poetry were common in that time

    b. talking about new types of poems each paragraph and explaining them a little

    c. focusing on one poet or group of people and the poems they wrote

    d. explaining older types of poetry so she can talk about modern poetry

29. The author's claim that poetry has been around "virtually from the time civilizations invented the written word" is supported by the detail that

    a. Beowulf is written in Old English, which is not really in use any longer

    b. epic poems told stories about heroes

    c. the Renaissance poets tried to copy Greek poets

    d. the Mesopotamians are credited with both inventing the word and writing "Epic of Gilgamesh"

30. According to the passage, the word that the word "telling" means

    a. speaking

    b. significant

    c. soothing

    d. wordy

MATHEMATICS

1. Brad has agreed to buy everyone a Coke. Each drink costs $1.89, and there are 5 friends. Estimate Brad's cost.

    a. $7
    b. $8
    c. $10
    d. $12

2. Estimate 215 x 65.

    a. 1,350
    b. 13,500
    c. 103,500
    d. 3,500

3. Sarah weighs 25 pounds more than Tony does. If together they weigh 205 pounds, how much will Sarah weigh approximately in kilograms? Assume 1 pound = 0.4535 kilograms.

    a. 41
    b. 48
    c. 50
    d. 52

4. Divide 243 by 3^3

    a. 243
    b. 11
    c. 9
    d. 27

5. **What fraction of $1500 is $75?**

    a. 1/14
    b. 3/5
    c. 7/10
    d. 1/20

6. **2/3 – 2/5 =**

    a. 4/10
    b. 1/15
    c. 3/7
    d. 4/15

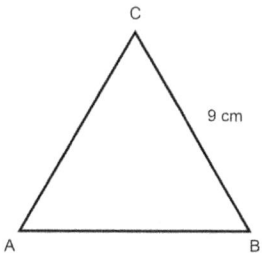

Note: figure not drawn to scale

7. **What is the perimeter of the equilateral △ABC above?**

    a. 18 cm
    b. 12 cm
    c. 27 cm
    d. 15 cm

8. Express 0.27 + 0.33 as a fraction.

   a. 3/6
   b. 4/7
   c. 3/5
   d. 2/7

9. $7^5 - 3^5$ =

   a. 15,000
   b. 16,564
   c. 15,800
   d. 15,007

10. What is 2/4 X 3/4 reduced to lowest terms?

    a. 6/12
    b. 3/8
    c. 6/16
    d. 3/4

11. Solve the following equation 4(y + 6) = 3y + 30

    a. y = 20
    b. y = 6
    c. y = 30/7
    d. y = 30

12. 2/3 of 60 + 1/5 of 75 =

    a. 45
    b. 55
    c. 15
    d. 50

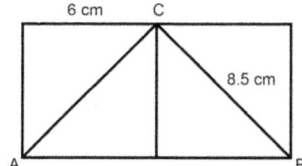

Note: figure not drawn to scale

13. Assuming the 2 quadrangles are identical rectangles, what is perimeter of △ABC in the above shape?

    a. 25.5 cm
    b. 27 cm
    c. 30 cm
    d. 29 cm

14. What is (3.13 + 7.87) X 5?

    a. 65
    b. 50
    c. 45
    d. 55

15. Solve for x if, $10^2 \times 100^2 = 1000^x$

    a. x = 2
    b. x = 3
    c. x = -2
    d. x = 0

16. What is 1/3 of 3/4?

   a. 1/4
   b. 1/3
   c. 2/3
   d. 3/4

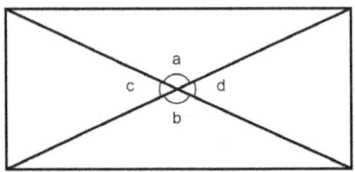

17. What is the sum of all the angles in the rectangle above?

   a. 180°
   b. 360°
   c. 90°
   d. 120°

18. Express 5 x 5 x 5 x 5 x 5 x 5 in exponential form.

   a. 5^6
   b. 10^6
   c. 5^{16}
   d. 5^3

19. Express 9 x 9 x 9 in exponential form and standard form.

   a. $9^3 = 719$
   b. $9^3 = 629$
   c. $9^3 = 729$
   d. $10^3 = 729$

20. If y = 4 and x = 3, solve yx^3

   a. -108
   b. 108
   c. 27
   d. 4

21. Divide 0.524 by 10^3

   a. 0.0524
   b. 0.00052
   c. 0.00524
   d. 524

22. If X = 7 solve 3x + 5 − 2x

   a. x = 6
   b. x = 12
   c. x = 1
   d. x = 0

23. (x − 2) / 4 − (3x + 5) / 7 = −3, x=?

   a. 6
   b. 7
   c. 10
   d. 13

24. 2/7 + 2/3 =

   a. 12/23
   b. 5/10
   c. 20/21
   d. 6/21

25. $3^2 \times 3^5$

    a. 3^{17}
    b. 3^5
    c. 4^8
    d. 3^7

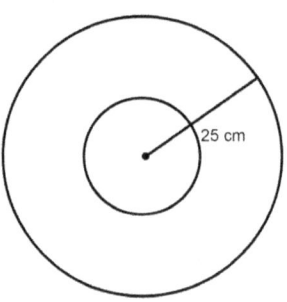

26. What is the distance traveled by the wheel above, if it makes 175 revolutions?

    a. 87.5 π m
    b. 875 π m
    c. 8.75 π m
    d. 8750 π m

27. Expand (x + 7)(x - 3)

    a. $x^2 + 4x - 21$
    b. x + 21
    c. 2x + 4 − 21
    d. 6x - 21 2x + 4x - 21

28. Estimate 2009 x 108.

    a. 110,000
    b. 2,0000
    c. 21,000
    d. 210,000

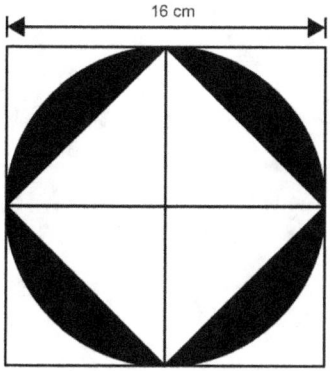

Note: figure not drawn to scale

29. A tile factory makes custom tiles, shown above, from two types of stone. If a customer requires 200 tiles, how much black stone will be required?

    a. 256 m²
    b. 2560 m²
    c. 2.56 m²
    d. 25.6 m²

30. Multiply 0.27 by 9^2

    a. 218.7
    b. 21.87
    c. 21
    d. 20.87

31. A woman spent 15% of her income on an item and ends with $120. What percentage of her income is left?

    a. 12%
    b. 85%
    c. 75%
    d. 95%

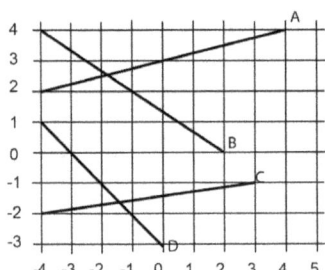

32. Which of the lines above represents the equation 2y − x = 4?

    a. A
    b. B
    c. C
    d. D

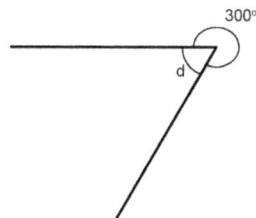

33. What is the measurement of the indicated angle?

    a. 45°
    b. 90°
    c. 60°
    d. 50°

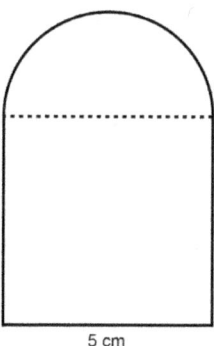

5 cm

Note: figure not drawn to scale

34. What is the perimeter of the above shape?

    a. 22.85 cm
    b. 20 cm
    c. 15 cm
    d. 25.546 cm

35. Solve $3^8/3^5$

    a. 3^3
    b. 3^5
    c. 3^6
    d. 3^4

36. Solve $3x - 27 = 0$

    a. $x = 24$
    b. $x = 30$
    c. $x = 9$
    d. $x = 21$

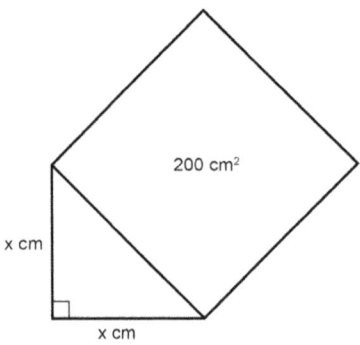

Note: Figure not drawn to scale

37. Assuming the quadrangle in the figure above is square, what is the length of the sides in the triangle above?

    a. 10
    b. 20
    c. 100
    d. 40

38. Solve 3b - 4 + 5b = 0

   a. b = 1
   b. b = 1/3
   c. b = 2
   d. b = 1/2

39. 3.14 + 2.73 + 23.7 =

   a. 28.57
   b. 30.57
   c. 29.56
   d. 29.57

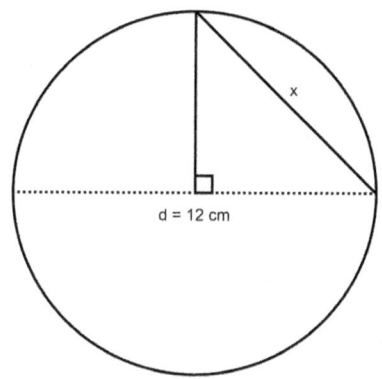

Note: Figure not drawn to scale

40. Calculate the length of side x.

   a. 6.46
   b. 8.48
   c. 3.6
   d. 6.4

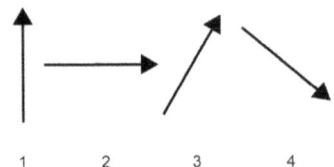

1   2   3   4

41. What is the correct order of respective slopes for the lines above?

    a. Positive, undefined, negative, positive
    b. Negative, zero, undefined, positive
    c. Undefined, zero, positive, negative
    d. Zero, positive undefined, negative

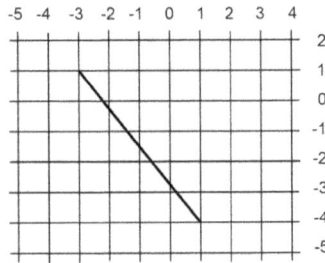

42. What is the slope of the line shown above?

    a. 5/4
    b. -4/5
    c. -5/4
    d. -4/5

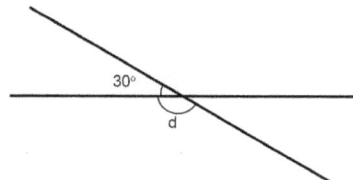

43. What is the indicated angle above?

    a. 150°
    b. 330°
    c. 60°
    d. 120°

44. Convert 16 quarts to gallons.

    a. 1 gallons
    b. 8 gallons
    c. 4 gallons
    d. 4.5 gallons

45. Convert 45 kg. to pounds.

    a. 10 pounds
    b. 100 pounds
    c. 1,000 pounds
    d. 110 pounds

46. 5x + 2(x + 7) = 14x – 7. Find x

   a. 1
   b. 2
   c. 3
   d. 4

47. 5(z + 1) = 3(z + 2) + 11. Find z

   a. 2
   b. 4
   c. 6
   d. 12

48. The price of a book went from $20 to $25. What percent did the price increase?

   a. 5%
   b. 10%
   c. 20%
   d. 25%

49. A boy is given 2 apples while his sister is given 8 oranges. What is the ratio between the boy's apples and her oranges?

   a. 1:2
   b. 2:4
   c. 1:4
   d. 2:1

50. In the time required to serve 43 customers, a server breaks 2 glasses and slips 5 times. The next day, the same server breaks 10 glasses. Assuming that glasses broken is proportional to customers served, how many customers did she serve?

   a. 25
   b. 43
   c. 86
   d. 215

51. A square lawn has an area of 62,500 square meters. What is the cost of building fence around it at a rate of $5.5 per meter?

   a. $4000
   b. $4500
   c. $5000
   d. $5500

52. Solve for n, when 5n + (19 – 2) = 67.

   a. 21
   b. 10
   c. 15
   d. 7

53. A distributor purchased 550 kilograms of potatoes for $165. He distributed these at a rate of $6.4 per 20 kilograms to 15 shops, $3.4 per 10 kilograms to 12 shops and the remainder at $1.8 per 5 kilograms. If his total distribution cost is $10, what will his profit be?

   a. $10.40
   b. $8.60
   c. $14.90
   d. $23.40

54. How much pay does Mr. Johnson receive if he gives half of his pay to his family, $250 to his landlord, and has exactly 3/7 of his pay left over?

   a. $3600
   b. $3500
   c. $2800
   d. $1750

55. In a store, the price of t-shirts and trousers are constant. If John buys 4 t-shirts and 5 trousers, he pays $51. If he buys 7 t-shirts and 3 trousers, then he pays $49. Find the difference between the price of one trousers and one t-shirt.

   a. 0
   b. 1 3
   c. 7
   d. 12

56. A number is increased by 2 and then multiplied by 3. The result is 24. What is this number?

   a. 4
   b. 6
   c. 8
   d. 10

57. My father's age divided by 5 is equal to my brother's age divided by 3. My brother is 3 years older than me. My father's age is 3 less than 2 times my age. How old is my father?

   a. 34
   b. 45
   c. 56

d. 61

58. Jane is three times Peter's age. When Peter is at Jane's age, Jane will be 8 less than 2 times Peter's age. Find the sum of Jane and Peter's age at present.

   a. 18
   b. 21
   c. 25
   d. 32

59. The sum of two numbers is 20 and their product is 91. Find the smaller number.

   a. 5
   b. 7
   c. 14
   d. 15

60. John's father is 6 times and 12 years older than John. When John will be at his father's age, his father will be 2 times and 3 less than John. How old is John today?

   a. 3
   b. 5
   c. 12
   d. 15

Mechanical Comprehension

1. Which of the following is an example of torque?

    a. The wheel of a pulley turning
    b. A piston moving
    c. A horse pulling a load
    d. A tow truck pulling a vehicle

2. Find the weight of load L in N, if the pulling force F = 20N.

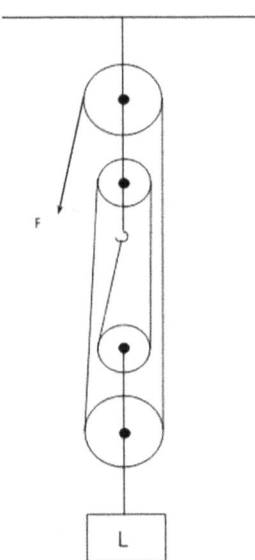

    a. 5
    b. 100
    c. 20
    d. 80

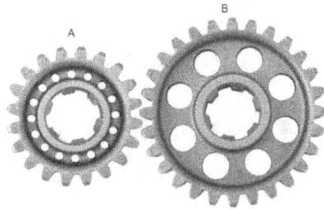

3. How many turns does the gear B make when the gear A makes 14 complete turns?

    a. 8
    b. 10
    c. 20
    d. 28

4. Which of the following is true about the system of meshed gears shown?

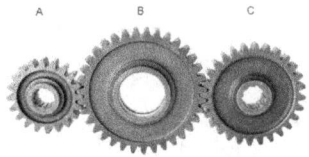

    a. Gear A rotates slower than gear B
    b. Gear A rotates slower than gear C
    c. Gear B rotates slower than gear C
    d. Gear B rotates faster than the other two gears

5. Which of the following is true of the relationship between screws and threads?

    a. The larger the distance between threads, the easier to turn.

    b. The smaller the distance between threads, the easier to turn.

    c. The smaller the distance between threads, the more difficult to turn.

    d. None of the above

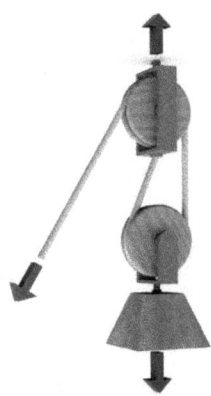

6. Consider the arrangement of pulleys above. If the weight shown is 150 pounds, how much force much be exerted to lift the weight?

    a. 150 pounds

    b. 100 pounds

    c. 75 pounds

    d. 50 pounds

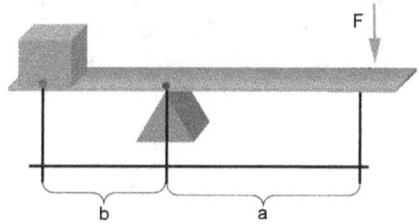

7. Consider the illustration above and the corresponding data:

Weight = W = 100 pounds
Distance from fulcrum to Weight = b = 5 feet
Distance from fulcrum to point where force is applied = a = 10 feet
How much force (F) must be applied to lift the weight?

    a. 100
    b. 50
    c. 25
    d. 10

8. Consider a gear train with 3 gears, from left to right, A with 10 teeth, gear B with 40 teeth, and gear C with 10 teeth. Gear A turns clockwise at 80 rpm. What direction and speed in rpm does Gear C turn?

    a. 100 rpm, clockwise
    b. 80 rpm clockwise
    c. 120 rpm counter clockwise
    d. 100 rpm counter clockwise

9. A force of 40 kg. is applied to two springs in parallel, which compresses the springs 10 inches. If the same force is applied to springs in series, how far will the springs compress?

    a. 40 inches
    b. 5 inches
    c. 10 inches
    d. 5 inches

10. Tension of 40 kg. is applied to two springs in series, which expand the springs 20 inches. If the same amount of tension is applied to springs in parallel, how far will the springs expand?

    a. 20 inches
    b. 10 inches
    c. 5 inches
    d. 2 inch

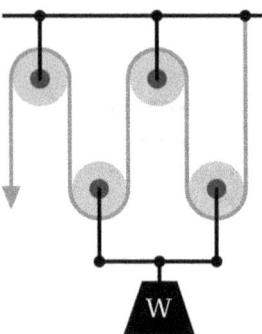

11. Consider the pulley arrangement above. If the weight, W, is 100 pounds, then how much force is required to lift the weight?

    a. 100 pounds
    b. 50 pounds
    c. 25 pounds
    d. 20 pounds

12. A cam is a mechanical linkage that:

a. Transforms linear motion into rotary motion and vice versa.

b. Transforms oscillating motion in to linear motion and vice versa.

c. Transforms reciprocating motion to oscillating motion.

d. None of the above

13. What is the function of the crankshaft?

a. To transform the back-and-forth motion of the pistons into rotary motion.

b. To transform rotary motion into reciprocal motion.

c. To transfer the rotary motion of the cam to the wheels

d. None of the above.

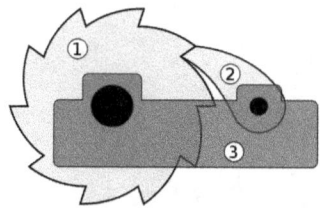

14. Identify the components labelled above.

a. 1 - ratchet, 2 - pawl, 3 - base

b. 1 - pawl, 2 - ratchet, 3 - base

c. 1 - gear, 2 - stop, 3 base

d. None of the above

15. Which equation below shows the relationship between F and P for the system of pulleys shown?

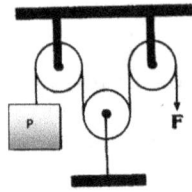

a. P = 3F
b. P = 2F
c. P = F
d. P = F/2

16. How many newtons of force is needed to pull the object up an inclined plane, if the weight of the object is 200 N?

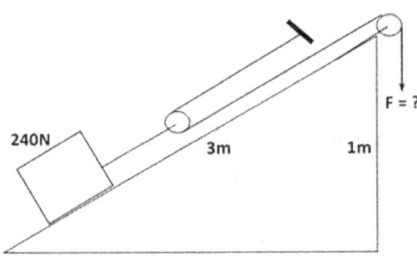

a. 50
b. 100
c. 150
d. 200

17. What is the force applied to lift the 400 N weight shown?

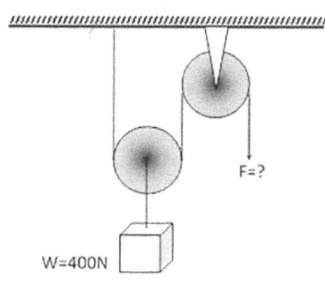

a. 200 N
b. 300 N
c. 400 N
d. 800 N

18. How many turns does gear 1 make when gear 3 makes 210 turns?

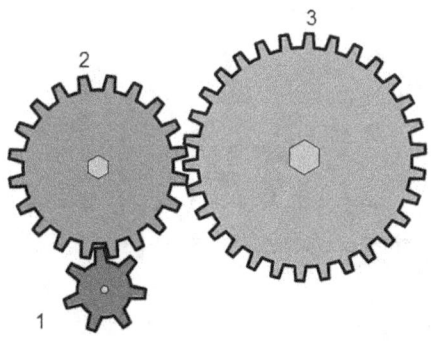

a. 30
b. 90
c. 300
d. 900

19. What is the minimum force (in N) needed to lift the 600 N object, if x = 3 m and y = 2 m?

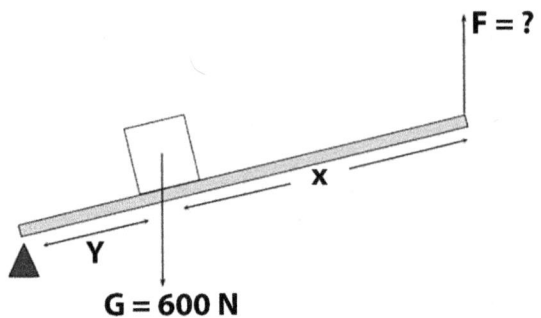

a. 400
b. 320
c. 240
d. 180

20. What is the distance between the mass m and the fulcrum, if the system is in equilibrium and the length of the rod d is 120 cm? Give the answer in cm.

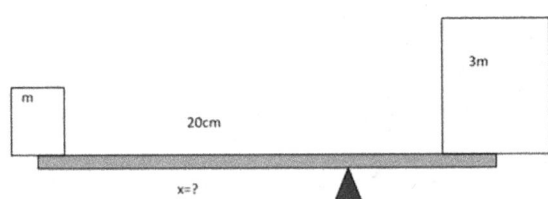

a. 80
b. 85
c. 90
d. 95

Answer Key

1. A
The correct answer because that fact is stated directly in the passage. The passage explains that Anne taught Helen to hear by allowing her to feel the vibrations in her throat.

2. B
We can infer that Anne is a patient teacher because she did not leave or lose her temper when Helen bit or hit her; she just kept trying to teach Helen. Choice B is incorrect because Anne taught Helen to read and talk. Choice C is incorrect because Anne could hear. She was partially blind, not deaf. Choice D is incorrect because it does not have to do with patience.

3. A
The passage states that it was hard for anyone but Anne to understand Helen when she spoke. Choice A is incorrect because the passage does not mention Helen spoke a foreign language. Choice C is incorrect because there is no mention of how quiet or loud Helen's voice was. Choice D is incorrect because we know from reading the passage that Helen did learn to speak.

4. B
This question tests the reader's summarization skills. The other choices A, B, and C focus on portions of the second paragraph that are too narrow and do not relate to the specific portion of text in question. The complexity of the sentence may mislead students into selecting one of these answers, but rearranging or restating the sentence will lead the reader to the correct answer. In addition, choice A makes an assumption that may or may not be true about the intentions of the company, choice B focuses on one product rather than the idea of the products, and choice C makes an assumption about women that may or may not be true and is not supported by the text.

5. D
This question tests the reader's summarization skills. The question is asking very generally about the message of the

passage, and the title, "Ways Characters Communicate in Theater," is one indication of that. The other choices A, B, and C are all directly from the text, and therefore readers may be inclined to select one of them, but are too specific to encapsulate the entirety of the passage and its message.

6. B
The paragraph on soliloquies mentions "To be or not to be," and it is from the context of that paragraph that readers may understand that because "To be or not to be" is a soliloquy, Hamlet will be introspective, or thoughtful, while delivering it. It is true that actors deliver soliloquies alone, and may be "solitary" (choice A), but "thoughtful" (choice B) is more true to the overall idea of the paragraph. Readers may choose C because drama and theater can be used interchangeably and the passage mentions that soliloquies are unique to theater (and therefore drama), but this answer is not specific enough to the paragraph in question. Readers may pick up on the theme of life and death and Hamlet's true intentions and select that he is "hopeless" (choice D), but those themes are not discussed either by this paragraph or passage, as a close textual reading and analysis confirms.

7. C
This question tests the reader's grammatical skills. Choice B seems logical, but parenthesis are actually considered to be a stronger break in a sentence than commas are, and along this line of thinking, actually disrupt the sentence more.

Choices A and D make comparisons between theater and film that are simply not made in the passage, and may or may not be true. This detail does clarify the statement that asides are most unique to theater by adding that it is not completely unique to theater, which may have been why the author didn't chose not to delete it and instead used parentheses to designate the detail's importance (choice C).

8. A
Low blood sugar occurs both in diabetics and healthy adults.

9. B
None of the statements are the author's opinion.

10. A
The author's purpose is the inform.

11. A
The only statement that is not a detail is, "A doctor can diagnosis this medical condition by asking the patient questions and testing."

12. A
This sentence is a recommendation.

13. C
Tips for a good night's sleep is the best alternative title for this article.

14. B
Mental activity is helpful for a good night's sleep is cannot be inferred from this article.

15. A
From the passage, one disadvantage of taking naps is they may keep you awake at night.

16. C
You would you find information about natural selection and adaptation page 110.

17. C
To be infamous means to be remembered for an evil or terrible action. Therefore, the word infamy means to remember a bad or terrible thing. Choice A is incorrect because being famous is not the same as being infamous. Choice B is incorrect because the attack on Pearl Harbor was not good. Choice D is incorrect because Pearl Harbor was not forgotten.

18. C
Each answer choice except choice C contains the name of at least one country that was not part of the AXIS powers.

19. D
It is stated in the passage. Choice A is not correct because there was no indication that Japan would attack San Diego. Choice B is incorrect because the attack on Pearl Harbor

was a surprise. Choice C is incorrect because Roosevelt was not planning to attack Japan.

20. C
The passage clearly states that Japan planned a surprise attack. They chose that early time to catch the U.S. military off guard. Choice A is incorrect because the military does not sleep late. Choice B is incorrect because there is no law against bombing countries. Choice D is incorrect because it makes no sense.

21. C
This question tests the reader's vocabulary skills. The uses of the negatives "but" and "less," especially right next to each other, may confuse readers into answering with choices A or D, which list words that are antonyms to "militant." Readers may also be confused by the comparison of healthy people with what is being described as an overly healthy person--both people are good, but the reader may look for which one is "worse" in the comparison, and therefore stray toward the antonym words. The key to understanding the meaning of "militant" is to look at the root of the word; readers can then easily associate it with "military" and gain a sense of what the word signifies: defence (especially considered that the immune system defends the body). Choice C is correct over choice B because "militant" is an adjective, just as the words in choice C are, whereas the words in choice B are nouns.

22. C
This question tests the reader's understanding of function within writing. The other choices are details included surrounding the quoted text, and may therefore confuse the reader. A somewhat contradicts what is said earlier in the paragraph, which is that tests and treatments are improving, and probably doctors are along with them, but the paragraph doesn't actually mention doctors, and the subject of the question is the medicine. Choice B may seem correct to readers who aren't careful to understand that, while the author does mention the large number of people affected, the author is touching on the realities of living with allergies rather than about the likelihood of curing all allergies. Similarly, while the author does mention the "balance" of the body, which is easily associated with "wholesome," the

author is not really making an argument and especially is not making an extreme statement that allergy medicines should be outlawed. Again, because the article's tone is on living with allergies, choice C is an appropriate choice that fits with the title and content of the text.

23. B
This question tests the reader's inference skills. The text does not state who is doing the recommending, but the use of the "patients," as well as the general context of the passage, lends itself to the logical partner, "doctors," choice B. The author does mention the recommendation but doesn't present it as her own (i.e. "I recommend that"), so choice A may be eliminated. It may seem plausible that people with allergies (choice D) may recommend medicines or products to other people with allergies, but the text does not necessarily support this interaction taking place. Choice C may be selected because the EpiPen is specifically mentioned, but the use of the phrase "such as" when it is introduced is not limiting enough to assume the recommendation is coming from its creators.

24. D
This question tests the reader's global understanding of the text. Choice D includes the main topics of the three body paragraphs, and isn't too focused on a specific aspect or quote from the text, as the other questions are, giving a skewed summary of what the author intended. The reader may be drawn to choice B because of the title of the passage and the use of words like "better," but the message of the passage is larger and more general than this.

25. B
Reading the document posted to the Human Resources website is optional.

26. B
The document is recommended changes and have not be implemented yet.

27. C

This question tests the reader's summarization skills. The use of the word "actually" in describing what kind of people poets are, as well as other moments like this, may lead readers to selecting Choices B or D, but the author is more information than trying to persuade readers. The author gives no indication that she loves poetry (choice B) or that people, students specifically (D), should write poems. Choice A is incorrect because the style and content of this paragraph do not match those of a foreword; forewords usually focus on the history or ideas of a specific poem to introduce it more fully and help it stand out against other poems. The author here focuses on several poems and gives broad statements. Instead, she tells a kind of story about poems, giving three very broad time periods in which to discuss them, thereby giving a brief history of poetry, as choice C states.

28. A

This question tests the reader's summarization skills. Key words in the topic sentences of each of the paragraphs ("oldest," "Renaissance," "modern") should give the reader an idea that the author is moving chronologically. The opening and closing sentence-paragraphs are broad and talk generally. B seems reasonable, but epic poems are mentioned in two paragraphs, eliminating the idea that only new types of poems are used in each paragraph. Choice C is also easily eliminated because the author clearly mentions several different poets, groups of people, and poems. Choice D also seems reasonable, considering that the author does move from older forms of poetry to newer forms, but use of "so (that)" makes this statement false, for the author gives no indication that she is rushing (the paragraphs are about the same size) or that she prefers modern poetry.

29. D

This question tests the reader's attention to detail. The key word is "invented"--it ties together the Mesopotamians, who invented the written word, and the fact that they, as the inventors, also invented and used poetry. The other selections focus on other details mentioned in the passage, such as that the Renaissance's admiration of the Greeks (choice C) and that Beowulf is in Old English (choice A). Choice B may seem like an attractive answer because it is unlike the others and because the idea of heroes seems rooted in ancient and early civilizations.

30. B
This question tests the reader's vocabulary and contextualization skills. "Telling" is not an unusual word, but it may be used here in a way that is not familiar to readers, as an adjective rather than a verb in gerund form. A may seem like the obvious answer to a reader looking for a verb to match the use they are familiar with. If the reader understands that the word is being used as an adjective and that choice A is a ploy, they may opt to select choice D, "wordy," but it does not make sense in context. Choice C can be easily eliminated, and doesn't have any connection to the paragraph or passage. "Significant" (choice B) makes sense contextually, especially relative to the phrase "give insight" used later in the sentence.

MATHEMATICS

1. C
If there are 5 friends and each drink costs $1.89, we can round up to $2 per drink and estimate the total cost at, 5 X $2 = $10.

The actual cost is 5 X $1.89 = $9.45.

2. B
Estimate 215 X 65. First start with 200 X 50, which is 10,000, so the answer will be about 10,000. The only choice that is close is 13,500, choice B.

3. D
Let us denote Sarah's weight by "x." Then, since she weighs 25 pounds more than Tony, Tony will be x-25. They together weigh 205 pounds which means that the sum of the two representations will be equal to 205:

Sarah : x

Tony : x - 25

x + (x - 25) = 205 ... by arranging this equation we have:

x + x - 25 = 205

2x - 25 = 205 ... we add 25 to each side to have x term alone:

2x - 25 + 25 = 205 + 25

2x = 230

x = 230/2

x = 115 pounds → Sarah weighs 115 pounds. Since 1 pound is 0.4535 kilograms, we need to multiply 115 by 0.4535 to have her weight in kilograms:

x = 115 * 0.4535 = 52.1525 kilograms → this is equal to 52 when rounded to the nearest whole number.

4. C
243/3^3 3 x 3 x 3 = 27
243/27 = 9

5. D
75/1500 = 15/300 = 3/60 = 1/20

6. D
2/3 - 2/5 = 10 - 6 /15 = 4/15

7. C
Equilateral triangle with 9 cm. sides
Perimeter = 9 + 9 + 9 = 27 cm.

8. C
0.27 + 0.33 = 0.60 and 0.60 = 60/100 = 3/5

9. B
(7 x 7 x 7 x 7 x 7) - (3 x 3 x 3 x 3 x 3) = 16,807 – 243 = 16,564

10. B
2/4 X 3/4 = 6/16, and reduced to the lowest terms = 3/8
11. B

$4y + 24 = 3y + 30$, $= 4y - 3y + 24 = 30$, $= y + 24 = 30$, $= y = 30 - 24$, $= y = 6$

12. B
$2/3 \times 60 = 40$ and $1/5 \times 75 = 15$, $40 + 15 = 55$.

13. D
Perimeter of triangle ABC is asked.
Perimeter of a triangle = sum of the three sides.

Here, Perimeter of ΔABC = |AC| + |CB| + |AB|.

Since the triangle is located in the middle of two adjacent and identical rectangles, we find the side lengths using these rectangles:

|AB| = 6 + 6 = 12 cm

|CB| = 8.5 cm

|AC| = |CB| = 8.5 cm

Perimeter = |AC| + |CB| + |AB| = 8.5 + 8.5 + 12 = 29 cm

14. D
$3.13 + 7.87 = 11$ and $11 \times 5 = 55$

15. A
$10 \times 10 \times 100 \times 100 = 1000^x$, $= 100 \times 10{,}000 = 1000^x$, $= 1{,}000{,}000 = 1000^x = x = 2$

16. A
$1/3 \times 3/4 = 3/12 = 1/4$

17. B
$a + b + c + d = ?$
The sum of angles around a point is 360°
$a + b + c + d = 360°$

18. A
5^6

19. C
Exponential form is 9^3 and standard from is 729

20. B
$(4)(3)^3 = (4)(27) = 108$

21. B
$0.524 / 10 \times 10 \times 10 = 0.524/1000 = 0.000524$

22. B
X = 7, so 3x = 3 x 7 = 21, 2x = 2 x 7 = 14, so 21 + 5 - 14 = 26 - 14 = 12

23. C
There are two fractions containing x and the denominators are different. First, let us find a common denominator to simplify the expression. The least common multiplier of 4 and 7 is 28. Then,
7(x – 2) / 28 – 4(3x + 5) / 28 = -3.28 / 28 ... Since both sides are written on the denominator 28 now, we can eliminate them:
7(x – 2) – 4(3x + 5) = -84
7x – 14 – 12x – 20 = -84
-5x = - 84 + 14 + 20
-5x = - 50
x = 50/5
x = 10

24. C
2/7 + 2/3 = 6+14 /21 (21 is the common denominator) = 20/21

25. D
When multiplying exponents with the same base, add the exponents. $3^2 \times 3^5 = 3^{2+5} = 3^7$

26. A
The wheel travels 2πr distance when it makes one revolution. Here, r stands for the radius. The radius is given as 25 cm in the figure. So,

2πr = 2π * 25 = 50π cm is the distance traveled in one revolution.

In 175 revolutions: 175 * 50π = 8750π cm is traveled.

We are asked to find the distance in meter.

Practice Test Questions 1

1 m = 100 cm So;

8750π cm = 8750π / 100 = 87.5π m

27. A
Multiply the first bracket and the second. $x^2 - 3x + 7x - 21 = x^2 + 4x - 21$

28. D
2009 X 108 = 216,972. This is an easy question to guess. 2000 X 100 = 200,000, so choices A, B and C can be eliminated right away.

29. A
Black stone for 200 tiles = 200 x [Total tile area – Inner white area(4 triangles)]
= 200 x [(16^2)-(4 x 1/2 x 8 x 8)] = 200 x (256 - 128) = 200 x 128 = 25600 cm²
Converting to meters – 1 cm. = 0.01 meters
= 25600/100 m²
= 256 m²

30. B
0.27 (9 x 9) = 0.27 x 81 = 21.87

31. B
She spent 15% - 100% - 15% = 85%

32. A
If a line represents an equation, all points on that line should satisfy the equation. Meaning that all (x, y) pairs present on the line should be able to verify that 2y - x is equal to 4. We can find out the correct line by trying a (x, y) point existing on each line. It is easier to choose points on the intersection of the grid lines:

Let us try the point (4, 4) on line A:

2 * 4 - 4 = 4

8 - 4 = 4

4 = 4 ... this is a correct result, so the equation for line A is

$2y - x = 4$.

Let us try other points to check the other lines:

Point (-1, 2) on line B:

$2 * 2 - (-1) = 4$

$4 + 1 = 4$

$5 = 4$ ... this is a wrong result, so the equation for line B is not $2y - x = 4$.

Point (3, -1) on line C:

$2 * (-1) - 3 = 4$

$-2 - 3 = 4$

$-5 = 4$ ... this is a wrong result, so the equation for line C is not $2y - x = 4$.

Point (-2, -1) on line D:

$2 * (-1) - (-2) = 4$

$-2 + 2 = 4$

$0 = 4$ ... this is a wrong result, so the equation for line D is not $2y - x = 4$.

33. C
The sum of angles around a point is 360°
$d + 300 = 360°$
$d = 60°$

34. A
Find the perimeter of a shape made by merging a square and a semi circle. Perimeter = 3 sides of the square + 1/2 circumference of the circle.
= (3 x 5) + 1/2 (5 π)
= 15 + 2.5 π
= 15 + 7.853975
Perimeter = 22.85 cm

Practice Test Questions 1

35. A

$3^{8-5} = 3^3$

To divide exponents with the same base, subtract the exponents.

36. C

$3x = 27$, $x = 27/3$, $x = 9$

37. A

If we call one side of the square "a," the area of the square will be a^2.

We know that $a^2 = 200$ cm².

On the other hand; there is an isosceles right triangle. Using the **Pythagorean Theorem:**

(Hypotenuse)² = (Adjacent Side)² + (Opposite Side)² Where the hypotenuse is equal to one side of the square. So,

$a^2 = x^2 + x^2$

$200 = 2x^2$

$200/2 = 2x^2/2$

$100 = x^2$

$x = \sqrt{100}$

$x = 10$ cm

38. D

$3b + 5b - 4$, $= 8b - 4$, $= 8b = 4$, $b = 4/8$, $= b = ½$

39. D

$3.14 + 2.73 = 5.87$ and $5.87 + 23.7 = 29.57$

40. B

In the question, we have a right triangle formed inside the circle. We are asked to find the length of the hypotenuse of this triangle. We can find the other two sides of the triangle by using circle properties:

The diameter of the circle is equal to 12 cm. The legs of the right triangle are the radii of the circle; so they are 6 cm long.

Using the Pythagorean Theorem:

(Hypotenuse)² = (Adjacent Side)² + (Opposite Side)²

$x^2 = r^2 + r^2$

$x^2 = 6^2 + 6^2$

$x^2 = 72$

$x = \sqrt{72}$

$x = 8.48$

41. C
Undefined, zero, positive, negative.

42. C
Slope (m) = change in y / change in x

$(x_1, y_1) = (-3, 1)$ & $(x_2, y_2) = (1, -4)$
Slope = [-4 - 1]/[1-(-3)] = -5/4

43. A
The angles opposite both angles 30° and angle d are respectively equal to vertical angles.
2(30° + d) = 360°
2d = 360° - 60°
2d = 300°
d = 150°

44. C
4 quarts = 1 gallon, 16 quarts = 16/4 = 4 gallons. Conversion problems are easy to get confused. One way to think of them is which is larger - quarts or gallons? Gallons are larger, so if you are converting from quarts to gallons the number of gallons will be a smaller number. Keeping that in mind, you can do a 'common-sense' check your answer.

45. B
0.45 kg = 1 pound, 1 kg. = 1/0.45 and 45 kg = 1/0.45 x 45 = 99.208, or 100 pounds.

46. C
To solve for x, first simplify the equation
5x + 2x + 14 = 14x − 7
7x - 14x = -14 -7
-7x = -21
x = -21/-7
x = 3

47. C
5z + 5 = 3z + 6 + 11
5z -3z + 5 = 6 + 11
5z − 3z = 6 + 11 -5
2z = 17 − 5
2z = 12
z = 12/2
z = 6

48. D
Price increased by $5 ($25-$20). To calculate the percent increase:
5/20 = X/100
500 = 20X
X = 500/20
X = 25%

49. C
The ratio is 2 to 8, or 1:4.

50. D
2 glasses are broken for 43 customers so 1 glass breaks for every 43/2 customers served, therefore 10 glasses implies (43/2) * 10 = 215 customers.

51. D
As the lawn is square, the length of one side will be the square root of the area. $\sqrt{62,500}$ = 250 meters. So, the perimeter is found by 4 times the length of the side of the square:

250 * 4 = 1000 meters.

Since each meter costs $5.5, the total cost of the fence will be 1000 * 5.5 = $5,500.

52. B

5n + (19 − 2) = 67, 5n + 17 = 67, 5n = 67 −17, 5n = 50, n = 50/5 = 10

53. B

The distribution is done in three different rates and amounts:

$6.4 per 20 kilograms to 15 shops ... 20 * 15 = 300 kilograms distributed

$3.4 per 10 kilograms to 12 shops ... 10 * 12 = 120 kilograms distributed

550 − (300 + 120) = 550 − 420 = 130 kilograms left. This amount is distributed by 5 kilogram portions. So, this means that there are 130/5 = 26 shops.

$1.8 per 130 kilograms.

We need to find the amount he earned overall these distributions.

$6.4 per 20 kilograms : 6.4 * 15 = $96 for 300 kilograms

$3.4 per 10 kilograms : 3.4 * 12 = $40.8 for 120 kilograms

$1.8 per 5 kilograms : 1.8 * 26 = $46.8 for 130 kilograms

So, he earned 96 + 40.8 + 46.8 = $ 183.6

The total distribution cost is given as $10

The profit is found by: Money earned − money spent ... It is important to remember that he bought 550 kilograms of potatoes for $165 at the beginning:

Profit = 183.6 − 10 − 165 = $8.6

54. B

We check the fractions taking place in the question. We see that there is a "half" (that is 1/2) and 3/7. So, we multiply the denominators of these fractions to decide how to name the total money. We say that Mr. Johnson has 14x at the beginning; he gives half of this, meaning 7x, to his family.

$250 to his landlord. He has 3/7 of his money left. 3/7 of 14x is equal to:

14x * (3/7) = 6x

So,

Spent money is: 7x + 250

Unspent money is: 6x

Total money is: 14x

We write an equation: total money = spent money + unspent money

14x = 7x + 250 + 6x

14x - 7x - 6x = 250

x = 250

We are asked to find the total money that is 14x:

14x = 14 * 250 = $3500

55. B

We have two variables: the price of a t-shirt and a trousers; and we have two situations given about them. We need to set two equations and solve them for the variables. Then, we are asked to find the difference between two.

Let us call the price of a t-shirt by a, and the price of a trousers by b:

If John buys 4 t-shirts and 5 trousers, he pays $51 → 4a + 5b = 51

If he buys 7 t-shirts and 3 trousers, then he pays $49 → 7a + 3b = 49

4a + 5b = 51

7a + 3b = 49

We have two paths to follow: substitution or elimination. Here, since extracting a or b from either of the equations result in fractions; it is easier to choose elimination:

-3/ 4a + 5b = 51

5/ 7a + 3b = 49

-12a - 15b = -153

35a + 15b = 245

23a = 92

a = 4

Choosing either of the equations, we can find b by inserting a:

4 . 4 + 5b = 51

16 + 5b = 51

5b = 35

b = 7

The difference between a and b is 7 - 4 = 3.

56. B

Let us call this number by x:

This number is increased by 2: x + 2

Then, it is multiplied by 3: 3(x + 2)

The result is 24: 3(x + 2) = 24 ... Solving this linear equation, we obtain the value of the number:

x + 2 = 24 / 3

x + 2 = 8

x = 8 – 2

$x = 6$

57. B

My age: x

My brother is 3 years older than me: $x + 3$

My father is 3 less than 2 times my age: $2x - 3$

My father's age divided by 5 is equal to my brother's age divided by 3: $(2x - 3) / 5 = (x + 3) / 3$

By cross multiplication:

$5(x + 3) = 3(2x - 3)$

$5x + 15 = 6x - 9$

$x = 24$

My father's age: $2.24 - 3 = 48 - 3 = 45$

58. D

Let us say that Peter is "a" years old today. Then, Jane is "3a". When Peter is "3a," $3a - a = 2a$ years will have passed and so, Jane will be $3a + 2a = 5a$. Then, we are given that Jane will be 8 less than 2 times Peter's age. So;

$5a = 2.3a - 8$

$5a = 6a - 8$

$a = 8$.

We are asked to find the sum of Jane and Peter's age at present.

Today, Peter is $a = 8$ years old and Jane is $3a = 24$ years old. Their sum is $8 + 24 = 32$.

59. B

We have two pieces of information provided. Using them, we will set an equation and solve it:

The sum of two numbers is 20; then one number is x and the other is 20 - x.

The product of these numbers is 91:

$x(20 - x) = 91$

$20x - x^2 = 91$

$x^2 - 20x + 91 = 0$

Using factorization method; notice that the multipliers of 91 that sum up to -20 are - 7 and - 13:

$(x - 13)(x - 7) = 0$

$x = 13$ and $x = 7$

This means that the two numbers are 7 and 13 and the smaller one is 7.

60. A

Let us denote John's age by x. Today, his father is 6x + 12 years old.

When John will be at his father's age, he will be 6x + 12 years old. This means that,

This will happen after $6x + 12 - x = 5x + 12$ years.

After 5x + 12 years, John's father will be $(6x + 12) + (5x + 12) = 11x + 24$ years old.

Now, let us set the equation related to the information that father will be 2 times and 3 less than John:

$11x + 24 = 2(6x + 12) - 3$

$11x + 24 = 12x + 24 - 3$

$x = 3$

Practice Test Questions 1

Mechanical Comprehension

1. A
The wheel of a pulley turning is an example of torque. Torque, is the tendency of a force to rotate an object about an axis, fulcrum, or pivot. Just as a force is a push or a pull, a torque can be thought of as a twist to an object.

2. D
The block and tackle system composed of a system of pulleys as shown operates according the following rule:

Pulling Force=Load/(Number of supporting ropes)
Here, the number of supporting ropes is 4. So, we have
20 = Load/4
So, Load = 20 × 4 = 80 N.

Do not confuse the number of supporting ropes. The rope, which is being pulled, is not counted. Otherwise, you will obtain the wrong answer, Choice B 100 (20 × 5).

3. B
The equation of meshed gears states that the speed of rotation V (in rot/s) is inversely proportional to the number of teeth N. Mathematically,

$V_A/V_B = N_B/N_A$

From the figure, it is obvious that N_A = 20 and N_B = 28. So, we have

$14/V_B = 28/20$

$V_B = (14 \times 20)/28 = 10$ turns

4. C
In meshed gears, larger the gear, slower the rotation and vice versa. Thus, gear B rotates slower than the others and gear A rotates the fastest.

5. B
The smaller the distance between threads, the easier to turn.

6. C
75 pounds of force much be exerted downward on the rope to lift the 150 pound weight.

7. B
To solve for F, Weight X b (distance from fulcrum to weight) = Force X a (distance from fulcrum to point where force is applied)
100 X 5 = F X 10
500/10 = F
F =50

8. B
First calculate the speed of gear B. The gear ratio is 10:40 or 1:4. If gear A is turning at 80 rpm, then gear B, which is larger, will turn slower, 80/4 = 20 rpm.

Next calculate B and C. Gear C is smaller, so it will turn faster. The gear ratio is 40:10 or 4:1, and since gear B turns at 20 rpm, gear C will turn at 20 X 4 = 80 rpm.

Next calculate the direction. Gear A is turning clockwise, so Gear B is turning counter clockwise, so Gear C must be turning clockwise.

9. B
If the springs in parallel compress 10 inches, then the springs in series will expand half that amount, or 5 inches.

10. B
If the springs in parallel expand 20 inches, then the springs in series will expand twice that amount, or 10 inches.

11. C
Notice the weight is attached to two of the pulleys. The weight required will therefore be 100/4 = 25 pounds.

12. B
A cam is a rotating or sliding piece in a mechanical linkage used especially in transforming rotary motion into linear motion or vice-versa

13. A
The function of the crankshaft is to transform the back-and-forth motion of the pistons into rotary motion.

14. A
The labelled components are, 1 - ratchet, 2 - pawl, 3 - base.

15. C
Here, there are 3 fixed pulleys forming a single system. It is known that fixed pulleys do not provide any gain in force. So, we have P = F

16. A
Here we have the combination of two systems composed of an inclined plane and a movable pulley.
The equation of the inclined plane is
Load/Force=(Path distance)/Height=Mechanical advantage

So, the mechanical advantage MA of the inclined plane is
MA = 2h/h = 2
The equation of the movable pulley is
Mechanical advantage= (Load)/(Force) = 2

Therefore, the total mechanical advantage is 2 × 2 = 4. This means the force needed to lift the 200 N weight is 200N / 4 = 50N (choice A).

17. A
Here, we have a system of combined pulley, i.e. one fixed and one movable. The fixed pulley does not provide any mechanical advantage while the movable pulley provides a mechanical advantage of 2.
So, the force required to lift the 400 N weight (load) is:
F = W/2 = 400N/2 = 200N

18. D
The equation of meshed gears states that the speed of rotation V (in rot/s) is inversely proportional to the number of teeth N. Mathematically,

$N_1 \cdot V_1 = N_2 \cdot V_2 = N_3 \cdot V_3$

Here, we are concerned only for the gears 1 and 3. Thus, we have
$7 \cdot V_1 = 30 \cdot 210$
$V_1 = (30 \cdot 210)/7 = 900$ turns

19. C
This is a second-class lever as the Load is between pivot and force.

The equation of levers is
Load × Load distance = Force × Force distance
Here, Load = G = 600N, Load distance = y = 2m, Force distance = x + y = 3m + 2m = 5m and calculate the force.
So,

600 X 2 = F X 5

F = (600 X 2)/5 = 1200/5 = 240N

20. C
This is an example of first-class lever as the pivot (fulcrum) is between Load and Force.

The equation of levers is
Load × Load distance = Force × Force distance

Here, Load = 3m · g, Force = m · g, Load distance = (120 – x) cm, and Force distance = x cm. Here, we have to calculate the force distance. So,

3mg × (120 - x) = mg × x

Simplifying mg from both sides, the equation becomes,

3 × (120 - x) = x

3 × 120 – 3 × x = x

4x = 360

X = 90cm

PRACTICE TEST QUESTIONS SET 2

THE PRACTICE TEST PORTION PRESENTS QUESTIONS THAT ARE REPRESENTATIVE OF THE TYPE OF QUESTION YOU SHOULD EXPECT TO FIND ON THE IRONWORKERS TEST. HOWEVER, THEY ARE NOT INTENDED TO MATCH EXACTLY WHAT IS ON THE IRONWORKERS TEST.

For the best results, take this Practice Test as if it were the real exam. Set aside time when you will not be disturbed, and a location that is quiet and free of distractions. Read the instructions carefully, read each question carefully, and answer to the best of your ability.

Use the bubble answer sheets provided. When you have completed the Practice Test, check your answer against the Answer Key and read the explanation provided.

Reading Comprehension

	A	B	C	D	E		A	B	C	D	E
1	○	○	○	○	○	21	○	○	○	○	○
2	○	○	○	○	○	22	○	○	○	○	○
3	○	○	○	○	○	23	○	○	○	○	○
4	○	○	○	○	○	24	○	○	○	○	○
5	○	○	○	○	○	25	○	○	○	○	○
6	○	○	○	○	○	26	○	○	○	○	○
7	○	○	○	○	○	27	○	○	○	○	○
8	○	○	○	○	○	28	○	○	○	○	○
9	○	○	○	○	○	29	○	○	○	○	○
10	○	○	○	○	○	30	○	○	○	○	○
11	○	○	○	○	○						
12	○	○	○	○	○						
13	○	○	○	○	○						
14	○	○	○	○	○						
15	○	○	○	○	○						
16	○	○	○	○	○						
17	○	○	○	○	○						
18	○	○	○	○	○						
19	○	○	○	○	○						
20	○	○	○	○	○						

MATHEMATICS & PROBLEM SOLVING

	A	B	C	D	E		A	B	C	D	E
1						31					
2						32					
3						33					
4						34					
5						35					
6						36					
7						37					
8						38					
9						39					
10						40					
11						41					
12						42					
13						43					
14						44					
15						45					
16						46					
17						47					
18						48					
19						49					
20						50					
21						51					
22						52					
23						53					
24						54					
25						55					
26						56					
27						57					
28						58					
29						59					
30						60					

Mechanical Comprehension

```
    A B C D
 1  ○ ○ ○ ○
 2  ○ ○ ○ ○
 3  ○ ○ ○ ○
 4  ○ ○ ○ ○
 5  ○ ○ ○ ○
 6  ○ ○ ○ ○
 7  ○ ○ ○ ○
 8  ○ ○ ○ ○
 9  ○ ○ ○ ○
10  ○ ○ ○ ○
11  ○ ○ ○ ○
12  ○ ○ ○ ○
13  ○ ○ ○ ○
14  ○ ○ ○ ○
15  ○ ○ ○ ○
16  ○ ○ ○ ○
17  ○ ○ ○ ○
18  ○ ○ ○ ○
19  ○ ○ ○ ○
20  ○ ○ ○ ○
```

Reading and Language Arts

Questions 1 - 4 refer to the following passage.

Passage 1 - The Crusades

In 1095 Pope Urban II proclaimed the First Crusade with the intent and stated goal to restore Christian access to holy places in and around Jerusalem. Over the next 200 years there were 6 major crusades and numerous minor crusades in the fight for control of the "Holy Land." Historians are divided on the real purpose of the Crusades, some believing that it was part of a purely defensive war against Islamic conquest; some see them as part of a long-running conflict at the frontiers of Europe; and others see them as confident, aggressive, papal-led expansion attempts by Western Christendom. The impact of the crusades was profound, and judgment of the Crusaders ranges from laudatory to highly critical. However, all agree that the Crusades and wars waged during those crusades were brutal and often bloody. Several hundred thousand Roman Catholic Christians joined the Crusades, they were Christians from all over Europe.

Europe at the time was under the Feudal System, so while the Crusaders made vows to the Church they also were beholden to their Feudal Lords. This led to the Crusaders not only fighting the Saracen, the commonly used word for Muslim at the time, but also each other for power and economic gain in the Holy Land. This infighting between the Crusaders is why many historians hold the view that the Crusades were simply a front for Europe to invade the Holy Land for economic gain in the name of the Church. Another factor contributing to this theory is that while the army of crusaders marched towards Jerusalem they pillaged the land as they went. The church and feudal Lords vowing to return the land to its original beauty, and inhabitants, this rarely happened though as the Lords often kept the land for themselves. A full 800 years after the Crusades, Pope John Paul II expressed his sorrow for the massacre of innocent people and the lasting damage the Medieval church caused in that area of the World.

1. What is the tone of this article?

a. Subjective
b. Objective
c. Persuasive
d. None of the Above

2. What can all historians agree on concerning the Crusades?

a. It achieved great things
b. It stabilized the Holy Land
c. It was bloody and brutal
d. It helped defend Europe from the Byzantine Empire

3. What impact did the feudal system have on the Crusades?

a. It unified the Crusaders
b. It helped gather volunteers
c. It had no effect on the Crusades
d. It led to infighting, causing more damage than good

4. What does Saracen mean?

a. Muslim
b. Christian
c. Knight
d. Holy Land

Practice Test Questions 2

Questions 5 - 8 refer to the following passage.

ABC Electric Warranty

ABC Electric Company warrants that its products are free from defects in material and workmanship. Subject to the conditions and limitations set forth below, ABC Electric will, at its option, either repair or replace any part of its products that prove defective due to improper workmanship or materials.

This limited warranty does not cover any damage to the product from improper installation, accident, abuse, misuse, natural disaster, insufficient or excessive electrical supply, abnormal mechanical or environmental conditions, or any unauthorized disassembly, repair, or modification.

This limited warranty also does not apply to any product on which the original identification information has been altered, or removed, has not been handled or packaged correctly, or has been sold as second-hand.

This limited warranty covers only repair, replacement, refund or credit for defective ABC Electric products, as provided above.

5. I tried to repair my ABC Electric blender, but could not, so can I get it repaired under this warranty?

    a. Yes, the warranty still covers the blender

    b. No, the warranty does not cover the blender

    c. Uncertain. ABC Electric may or may not cover repairs under this warranty

6. My ABC Electric fan is not working. Will ABC Electric provide a new one or repair this one?

    a. ABC Electric will repair my fan

    b. ABC Electric will replace my fan

    c. ABC Electric could either replace or repair my fan can request either a replacement or a repair.

7. My stove was damaged in a flood. Does this warranty cover my stove?

    a. Yes, it is covered.

    b. No, it is not covered.

    c. It may or may not be covered.

    d. ABC Electric will decide if it is covered

8. Which of the following is an example of improper workmanship?

    a. Missing parts

    b. Defective parts

    c. Scratches on the front

    d. None of the above

Questions 9 – 12 refer to the following passage.

Passage 2 - Women and Advertising

Only in the last few generations have media messages been so widespread and so readily seen, heard, and read by so many people. Advertising is an important part of both selling and buying anything from soap to cereal to jeans. For whatever reason, more consumers are women than are men. Media message are subtle but powerful, and more attention has been paid lately to how these message affect women.
Of all the products that women buy, makeup, clothes, and other stylistic or cosmetic products are among the most

popular. This means that companies focus their advertising on women, promising them that their product will make her feel, look, or smell better than the next company's product will. This competition has resulted in advertising that is more and more ideal and less and less possible for everyday women. However, because women do look to these ideals and the products they represent as how they can potentially become, many women have developed unhealthy attitudes about themselves when they have failed to become those ideals.

In recent years, more companies have tried to change advertisements to be healthier for women. This includes featuring models of more sizes and addressing a huge outcry against unfair tools such as airbrushing and photo editing. There is debate about what the right balance between real and ideal is, because fashion is also considered art and some changes are made to purposefully elevate fashionable products and signify that they are creative, innovative, and the work of individual people. Artists want their freedom protected as much as women do, and advertising agencies are often caught in the middle.

Some claim that the companies who make these changes are not doing enough. Many people worry that there are still not enough models of different sizes and different ethnicities. Some people claim that companies use this healthier type of advertisement not for the good of women, but because they would like to sell products to the women who are looking for these kinds of messages. This is also a hard balance to find: companies do need to make money, and women do need to feel respected.

While the focus of this change has been on women, advertising can also affect men, and this change will hopefully be a lesson on media for all consumers.

9. The second paragraph states that advertising focuses on women

       a. to shape what the ideal should be

       b. because women buy makeup

       c. because women are easily persuaded

       d. because of the types of products that women buy

10. According to the passage, fashion artists and female consumers are at odds because

    a. there is a debate going on and disagreement drives people apart

    b. both of them are trying to protect their freedom to do something

    c. artists want to elevate their products above the reach of women

    d. women are creative, innovative, individual people

11. The author uses the phrase "for whatever reason" in this passage to

    a. keep the focus of the paragraph on media messages and not on the differences between men and women

    b. show that the reason for this is unimportant

    c. argue that it is stupid that more women are consumers than men

    d. show that he or she is tired of talking about why media messages are important

12. This passage suggests that

    a. advertising companies are still working on making their messages better

    b. all advertising companies seek to be more approachable for women

    c. women are only buying from companies that respect them

    d. artists could stop producing fashionable products if they feel bullied

Questions 13 - 16 refer to the following passage.

FDR, the Treaty of Versailles, and the Fourteen Points

At the conclusion of World War I, those who had won the war and those who were forced to admit defeat welcomed the end of the war and expected that a peace treaty would be signed. The American president, Franklin D. Roosevelt, played an important part in proposing what the agreements should be and did so through his Fourteen Points.
World War I had begun in 1914 when an Austrian archduke was assassinated, leading to a domino effect that pulled the world's most powerful countries into war on a large scale. The war catalyzed the creation and use of deadly weapons that had not previously existed, resulting in a great loss of soldiers on both sides of the fighting. More than 9 million soldiers were killed.

The United States agreed to enter the war right before it ended, and many believed that its decision to become finally involved brought on the end of the war. FDR made it very clear that the U.S. was entering the war for moral reasons and had an agenda focused on world peace. The Fourteen Points were individual goals and ideas (focused on peace, free trade, open communication, and self reliance) that FDR wanted the power nations to strive for now that the war had concluded. He was optimistic and had many ideas about what could be accomplished through and during the post-war peace. However, FDR's fourteen points were poorly received when he presented them to the leaders of other world powers, many of whom wanted only to help their own countries and to punish the Germans for fuelling the war, and they fell by the wayside. World War II was imminent, for Germany lost everything.

Some historians believe that the other leaders who participated in the Treaty of Versailles weren't receptive to the Fourteen Points because World War I was fought almost entirely on European soil, and the United States lost much less than did the other powers. FDR was in a unique position to determine the fate of the war, but doing it on his own terms did not help accomplish his goals. This is only one historical example of how the United State has tried to use its power as an important country, but found itself limited because of geological or ideological factors.

13. The main idea of this passage is that

    a. World War I was unfair because no fighting took place in America

    b. World War II happened because of the Treaty of Versailles

    c. the power the United States has to help other countries also prevents it from helping other countries

    d. Franklin D. Roosevelt was one of the United States' smartest presidents

14. According to the second paragraph, World War I started because

    a. an archduke was assassinated

    b. weapons that were more deadly had been developed

    c. a domino effect of allies agreeing to help each other

    d. the world's most powerful countries were large

15. The author includes the detail that 9 million soldiers were killed

    a. to demonstrate why European leaders were hesitant to accept peace

    b. to show the reader the dangers of deadly weapons

    c. to make the reader think about which countries lost the most soldiers

    d. to demonstrate why World War II was imminent

16. According to this passage, the word catalyzed means

    a. analysed

    b. sped up

    c. invented

    d. funded

Questions 17 - 20 refer to the following passage.

Chocolate Chip Cookies

3/4 cup sugar
3/4 cup packed brown sugar
1 cup butter, softened
2 large eggs, beaten
1 teaspoon vanilla extract
2 1/4 cups all-purpose flour
1 teaspoon baking soda
3/4 teaspoon salt
2 cups semisweet chocolate chips
If desired, 1 cup chopped pecans, or chopped walnuts.
Preheat oven to 375 degrees.

Mix sugar, brown sugar, butter, vanilla and eggs in a large bowl. Stir in flour, baking soda, and salt. The dough will be very stiff.

Stir in chocolate chips by hand with a sturdy wooden spoon. Add the pecans, or other nuts, if desired. Stir until the chocolate chips and nuts are evenly dispersed.

Drop dough by rounded tablespoonfuls 2 inches apart onto a cookie sheet.

Bake 8 to 10 minutes or until light brown. Cookies may look underdone, but they will finish cooking after you take them out of the oven.

17. What is the correct order for adding these ingredients?

    a. Brown sugar, baking soda, chocolate chips
    b. Baking soda, brown sugar, chocolate chips
    c. Chocolate chips, baking soda, brown sugar
    d. Baking soda, chocolate chips, brown sugar

18. What does sturdy mean?

    a. Long
    b. Strong
    c. Short
    d. Wide

19. What does disperse mean?

    a. Scatter
    b. To form a ball
    c. To stir
    d. To beat

20. When can you stop stirring the nuts?

    a. When the cookies are cooked.
    b. When the nuts are evenly distributed.
    c. When the nuts are added.
    d. After the chocolate chips are added.

Questions 21 - 23 refer to the following passage.

Lowest Price Guarantee

Get it for less. Guaranteed!

ABC Electric will beat any advertised price by 10% of the difference.

> 1) If you find a lower advertised price, we will beat it by 10% of the difference.
>
> 2) If you find a lower advertised price within 30 days* of your purchase we will beat it by 10% of the difference.
>
> 3) If our own price is reduced within 30 days* of your purchase, bring in your receipt and we will refund the difference.

*14 days for computers, monitors, printers, laptops, tablets, cellular & wireless devices, home security products, projectors, camcorders, digital cameras, radar detectors, portable DVD players, DJ and pro-audio equipment, and air conditioners.

21. I bought a radar detector 15 days ago and saw an ad for the same model only cheaper. Can I get 10% of the difference refunded?

> a. Yes. Since it is less than 30 days, you can get 10% of the difference refunded.
>
> b. No. Since it is more than 14 days, you cannot get 10% of the difference re-funded.
>
> c. It depends on the cashier.
>
> d. Yes. You can get the difference refunded.

22. I bought a flat-screen TV for $500 10 days ago and found an advertisement for the same TV, at another store, on sale for $400. How much will ABC refund under this guarantee?

    a. $100
    b. $110
    c. $10
    d. $400

23. What is the purpose of this passage?

    a. To inform
    b. To educate
    c. To persuade
    d. To entertain

Questions 24 - 27 refer to the following passage.

Passage 6 - What Is Mardi Gras?

Mardi Gras is fast becoming one of the South's most famous and most celebrated holidays. The word Mardi Gras comes from the French and the literal translation is "Fat Tuesday." The holiday has also been called Shrove Tuesday, due to its associations with Lent. The purpose of Mardi Gras is to celebrate and enjoy before the Lenten season of fasting and repentance begins.

What originated by the French Explorers in New Orleans, Louisiana in the 17th century is now celebrated all over the world. Panama, Italy, Belgium and Brazil all host large scale Mardi Gras celebrations, and many smaller cities and towns celebrate this fun loving Tuesday as well. Usually held in February or early March, Mardi Gras is a day of extravagance, a day for people to eat, drink and be merry, to wear costumes, masks and to dance to jazz music.

The French explorers on the Mississippi River would be in shock today if they saw the opulence of the parades and floats that grace the New Orleans streets during Mardi Gras these days. Parades in New Orleans are divided by organizations. These are more commonly known as Krewes.

Being a member of a Krewe is quite a task because Krewes are responsible for overseeing the parades. Each Krewe's parade is ruled by a Mardi Gras "King and Queen." The role of the King and Queen is to "bestow" gifts on their adoring fans as the floats ride along the street. They throw doubloons, which is fake money and usually colored green, purple and gold, which are the colors of Mardi Gras. Beads in those color shades are also thrown and cups are thrown as well. Beads are by far the most popular souvenir of any Mardi Gras parade, with each spectator attempting to gather as many as possible.

24. The purpose of Mardi Gras is to

    a. Repent for a month.

    b. Celebrate in extravagant ways.

    c. Be a member of a Krewe.

    d. Explore the Mississippi.

25. From reading the passage we can infer that "Kings and Queens,"

    a. Have to be members of a Krewe.

    b. Have to be French.

    c. Have to know how to speak French.

    d. Have to give away their own money.

26. Which group of people began to hold Mardi Gras celebrations?

    a. Settlers from Italy

    b. Members of Krewes

    c. French explorers

    d. Belgium explorers

27. In the context of the passage, what does spectator mean?

    a. Someone who participates actively

    b. Someone who watches the parade's action

    c. Someone on the parade floats

    d. Someone who does not celebrate Mardi Gras

Questions 28 - 30 refer to the following passage.

Passage 1 - Caterpillars

Butterflies and moths have a three stage life cycle. Caterpillars are the first or laval stage. Caterpillars can be either herbivores, feeding mostly on plants, or carnivores, feeding on other insects. Caterpillars eat continuously. Once they are too big for their body, they shed or molt their skin.

Some caterpillars have symbiotic relationships with other insects. A symbiotic relationship is where different species work together in a way that is either harmful or helpful. Symbiotic relationships are critical to many species and ecosystems.

Some caterpillars and ants have a symbiotic or mutual relationship where both benefit. Ants give some protection, and caterpillars provide the ants with honeydew nectar.

Ants and caterpillars communicate by vibrations through the soil as well as grunting and squeaking. Humans are not able to hear these communications.

28. What do most larvae spend their time doing?

    a. Eating

    b. Sleeping

    c. Communicating with ants.

    d. None of the above

29. Are all caterpillars herbivores?

    a. Yes

    b. No, some eat insects

30. What benefit do larvae get from association with ants?

    a. They do not receive any benefit.
    b. Ants give them protection.
    c. Ants give them food.
    d. Ants give them honeydew secretions.

MATHEMATICS

1. Translate the following into an equation:

2 plus a number divided by 7.

    a. $(2 + X)/7$
    b. $(7 + X)/2$
    c. $(2 + 7)/X$
    d. $2/(7 + X)$

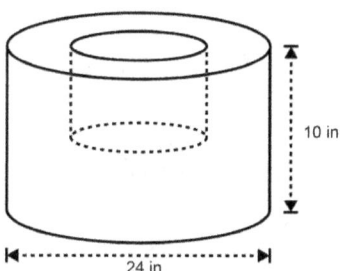

Note: figure not drawn to scale

2. What is the volume of the above solid made by a hollow cylinder that is half the size (in all dimensions) of the larger cylinder?

    a. 1440 π in³
    b. 1260 π in³
    c. 1040 π in³
    d. 960 π in³

3. If a train travels at 72 kilometers per hour, how far will it travel in 12 seconds?

    a. 200 m
    b. 220 m
    c. 240 m
    d. 260 m

4. Tony bought 15 dozen eggs for $80. 16 eggs were broken during loading and unloading. He sold the remaining eggs for $0.54 each. What will be his percent profit?

    a. 11%
    b. 11.2%
    c. 11.5%
    d. 12%

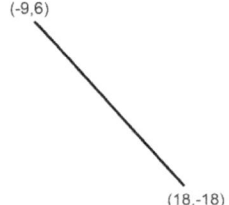

Practice Test Questions 2

5. What is the slope of the line above?

    a. -8/9
    b. 9/8
    c. -9/8
    d. 8/9

6. In a class of 83 students, 72 are present. What percent of students are absent?

    a. 12%
    b. 13%
    c. 14%
    d. 15%

7. $9ab^2 + 8ab^2 =$

    a. ab^2
    b. $17ab^2$
    c. 17
    d. $17a^2b^2$

8. The total expense of building a fence around a square shaped field is $2000 at a rate of $5 per meter. What is the length of one side?

    a. 80 meters
    b. 100 meters
    c. 40 meters
    d. 320 meters

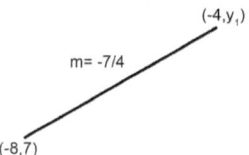

9. With the data given above, what is the value of y_1?

   a. 0
   b. -7
   c. 7
   d. 8

10. In a local election at polling station A, 945 voters cast their vote out of 1270 registered voters. At polling station B, 860 cast their vote out of 1050 registered voters and at station C, 1210 cast their vote out of 1440 registered voters. What was the total turnout including all three polling stations?

   a. 70%
   b. 74%
   c. 76%
   d. 80%

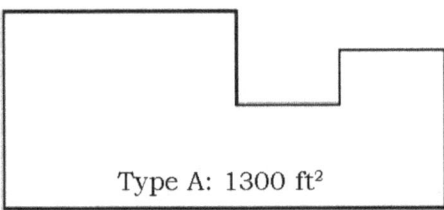

Type A: 1300 ft²

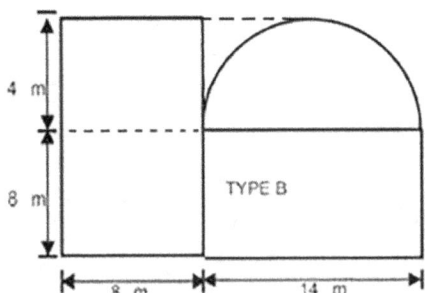

Note: Figure not drawn to scale

11. The price of houses in a certain subdivision is based on the total area. Susan is watching her budget and wants to choose the house with the lowest area. Which house type, A (1300 ft2) or B, should she choose if she would like the house with the lowest price? (1 m2 = 10.76 ft2 & π = 22/7)

    a. Type B is smaller at 140 ft²
    b. Type A is smaller
    c. Type B is smaller at 855 ft²
    d. Type B is larger

Consider the following graph.

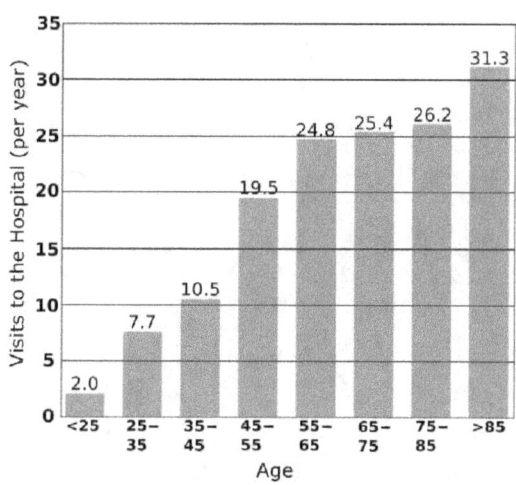

12. How many hospital visits per year does a person aged 85 or more make?

    a. 26.2
    b. 31.3
    c. More than 31.3
    d. A decision cannot be made from this graph.

13. Based on this graph, how many visits per year do you expect a person that is 95 or older to make?

    a. More than 31.3

    b. Less than 31.3

    c. 31.3

    d. A decision cannot be made from this graph.

14. How much water can be stored in a cylindrical container 5 meters in diameter and 12 meters high?

Note: figure not drawn to scale

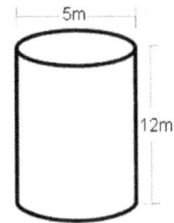

    a. 235.65 m³

    b. 223.65 m³

    c. 240.65 m³

    d. 252.65 m³

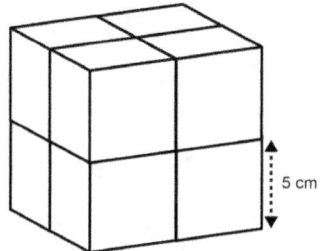

Note: figure not drawn to scale

15. Assuming the figure above has cubes, what is the volume?

    a. 125 cm³
    b. 875 cm³
    c. 1000 cm³
    d. 500 cm³

16. 1 gallon = _____ liter(s).

    a. 1 liter
    b. 3.785 liters
    c. 37.85 liters
    d. 4.5 liters

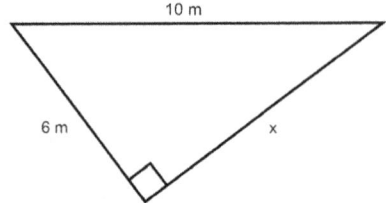

Note: figure not drawn to scale

17. What is the length of the missing side in the triangle above?

    a. 6
    b. 4
    c. 8
    d. 5

18. 60 is 75% of x. Solve for x.

    a. 80
    b. 90
    c. 75
    d. 70

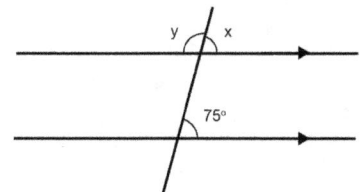

19. What is the value of the angle y?

   a. 25°
   b. 15°
   c. 30°
   d. 105°

20. Express 71/1000 as a decimal.

   a. .71
   b. .0071
   c. .071
   d. 7.1

21. .33 × .59 =

   a. .1947
   b. 1.947
   c. .0197
   d. .1817

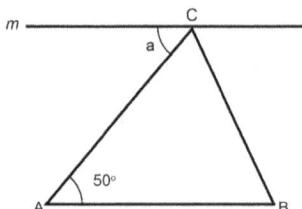

Note: Figure not drawn to scale

22. If the line *m* is parallel to the side AB of △ABC, what is angle *a*?

    a. 130°
    b. 25°
    c. 65°
    d. 50°

23. 7x − 9 = 47. Solve for x.

    a. 8
    b. 7
    c. 9
    d. 6

24. What number is in the ten thousandths place in 1.7389

    a. 1
    b. 8
    c. 9
    d. 3

25. .87 - .48 =

    a. .39
    b. .49
    c. .41
    d. .37

26. Which is the equivalent decimal number for forty nine thousandths?

    a. .49
    b. .0049
    c. .049
    d. 4.9

27. Which of the following is not a fraction equivalent to 3/4?

    a. 6/8
    b. 9/12
    c. 12/18
    d. 21/28

28. Which one of the following is greater than a third?

    a. 84/231
    b. 6/35
    c. 3/22
    d. b and c

29. Which of the following numbers is the greatest?

    a. 1
    b. $\sqrt{2}$
    c. 3/2
    d. 4/3

30. 2b + 9b − 5b = 0

    a. 3b
    b. 6b
    c. 4b
    d. 8b

31. $(4Y^3 - 2Y^2) + (7Y^2 + 3y - y) =$

    a. $4y^3 + 9y^2 + 4y$
    b. $5y^3 + 5y^2 + 3y$
    c. $4y^3 + 7y^2 + 2y$
    d. $4y^3 + 5y^2 + 2y$

32. 4.7 + .9 + .01 =

    a. 5.5
    b. 6.51
    c. 5.61
    d. 5.7

33. 7(2y + 8) + 1 − 4(y + 5) =

    a. 10y + 36
    b. 10y + 77
    c. 18y + 37
    d. 10y + 37

34. What is the distance between the two points?

    a. ≈19
    b. 20
    c. ≈21
    d. ≈22

35. 60% of x is 12. Solve for x.

    a. 18
    b. 15
    c. 25
    d. 20

36. .84 ÷ .7 =

    a. .12
    b. 12
    c. .012
    d. 1.2

37. 6(x − 4) = 3x + 12. Solve for x.

    a. 15
    b. 8
    c. 12
    d. 14

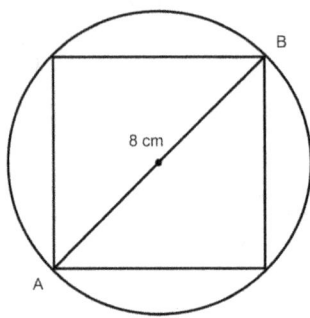

Note: figure not drawn to scale

38. What is area of the circle?

    a. 4 π cm²
    b. 12 π cm²
    c. 10 π cm²
    d. 16 π cm²

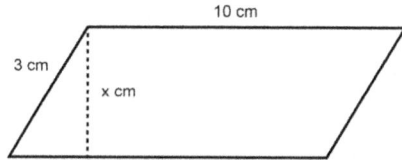

Note: figure not drawn to scale

39. What is the perimeter of the parallelogram above?

    a. 12 cm
    b. 26 cm
    c. 13 cm
    d. (13+x) cm

40. Richard gives 's' amount of salary to each of his 'n' employees weekly. If he has 'x' amount of money then how many days he can employ these 'n' employees.

    a. sx/7n
    b. 7x/nx
    c. nx/7s
    d. 7x/ns

41. Express 87% as a decimal.

    a. .087
    b. 8.7
    c. .87
    d. 87

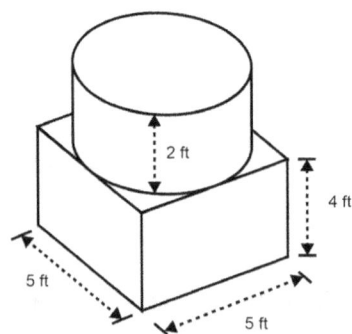

·Note: figure not drawn to scale

42. What is the approximate total volume of the above solid?

    a. 120 ft³
    b. 100 ft³
    c. 140 ft³
    d. 160 ft³

43. Susan wants to buy a leather jacket that costs $545.00 and is on sale for 10% off. What is the approximate cost?

    a. $525
    b. $450
    c. $475
    d. $500

44. Translate the following into an equation:

Five greater than 3 times a number.

    a. 3X + 5
    b. 5X + 3
    c. (5 + 3)X
    d. 5(3 + X)

45. What is the slope of the line above?

   a. 1
   b. 2
   c. 3
   d. -2

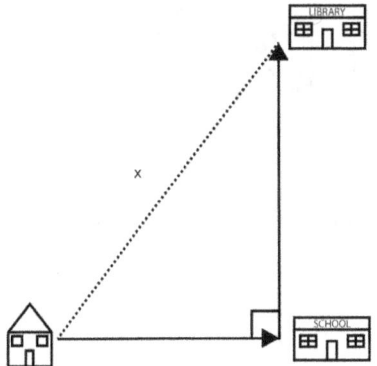

Note: figure not drawn to scale

46. Every day starting from his home Peter travels due east 3 kilometers to the school. After school he travels due north 4 kilometers to the library. What is the distance between Peter's home and the library?

   a. 15 km
   b. 10 km
   c. 5 km
   d. 12 ½ km

47. The cost of waterproofing canvas is .50 per square yard. What is the total cost for waterproofing a canvas truck cover that is 15' x 24'?

    a. $18.00
    b. $6.67
    c. $180.00
    d. $20.00

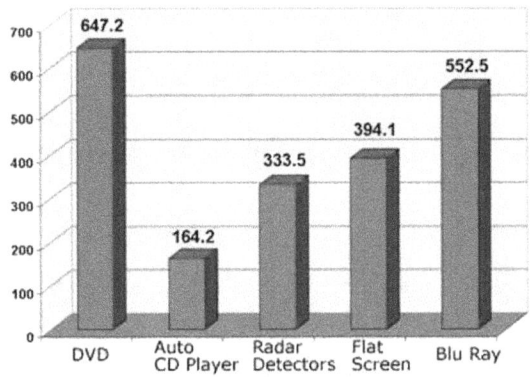

48. Consider the graph above. What is the third best-selling product?

    a. Radar Detectors
    b. Flat Screen TV
    c. Blu Ray
    d. Auto CD Players

49. Which two products are the closest in the number of sales?

    a. Blu Ray and Flat Screen TV
    b. Flat Screen TV and Radar Detectors
    c. Radar Detectors and Auto CD Players
    d. DVD players and Blu Ray

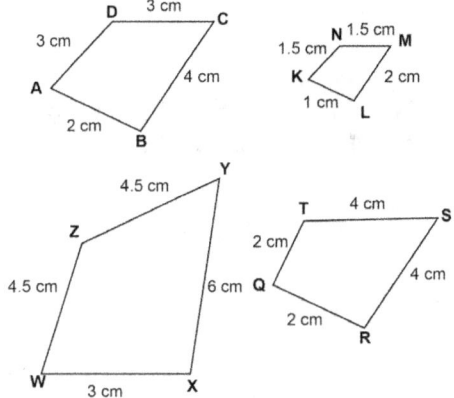

50. Which of the above quadrilaterals are similar?

    a. All are similar
    b. QRST, KLMN, WXYZ
    c. ABCD, KLMN, WXYZ
    d. None of the choices are correct.

Mechanical Comprehension

1. What is the value of the force F enough to lift the object up, if the weight W of the object is 360 N?

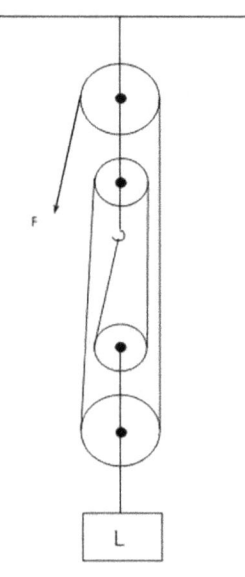

   a. 180 N
   b. 120 N
   c. 90 N
   d. 72 N

2. How many turns does the gear A make if the gear B makes 100 turns?

   a. 175
   b. 70
   c. 7
   d. 5

3. Which of the following statements about gears is false?

    a. Gears are teethed wheels used to generate rotation

    b. Meshed gears move at the same time

    c. Meshed gears move at the same speed

    d. Teeth in gears help increase the friction and avoid slipping

4. What direction does the rack in the figure move if the pinion rotates clockwise?

    a. Left
    b. Right
    c. Up
    d. Down

5. What direction does the pinion in the figure rotate if the rack shifts on the right?

    a. Clockwise
    b. Counter-clockwise
    c. First clockwise then counter-clockwise
    d. First counter-clockwise, then clockwise

6. The system shown is in equilibrium and the rod is weightless. What is the ratio P/F ?

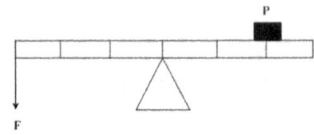

a. 3/2
b. 2/3
c. 1
d. 5/3

7. What is the ratio of the load to effort?

a. Torque
b. Mechanical Advantage
c. Energy
d. Mechanical Energy

8. Which type of lever does the wheel and axle system shown represent?

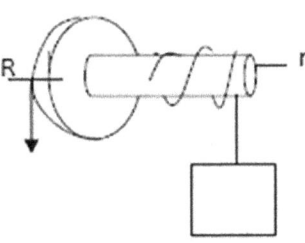

a. First class lever
b. Second class lever
c. Third class lever
d. Fourth class lever

9. What is the working principle of sugar tongs?

   a. First class lever
   b. Second class lever
   c. Third class lever
   d. Fourth class lever

10. Find the value of the ratio F/W, if R/r = 3.

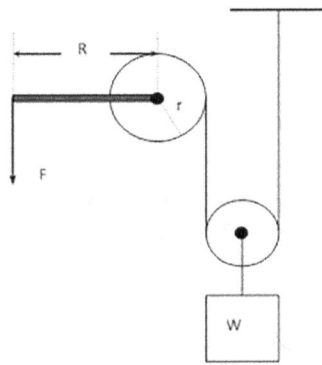

   a. 3
   b. 1/3
   c. 6
   d. 1/6

11. In the figure above $m_1 = 4$ kg and $m_2 = 2$ kg. What is the value of m_3 in kg if the system is in equilibrium? (The rod is weightless)

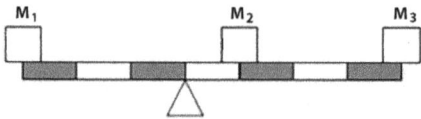

a. 2
b. 2.5
c. 3
d. 3.5

12. What is the reading of dynamo-meter in the figure below if the system is in equilibrium? The bar has no mass.

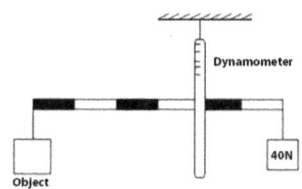

a. 20N
b. 40N
c. 60N
d. 80N

13. A uniform rod can be hold in equilibrium with the help of a system of pulleys as in the figure below. What is the weight of the rod if the force F = 3N?

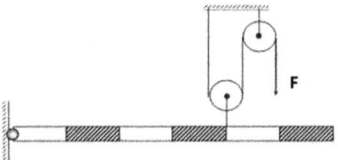

a. 3N
b. 4N
c. 6N
d. 8N

14. The length of the lever is 1 meter. What is the mechanical advantage of the system?

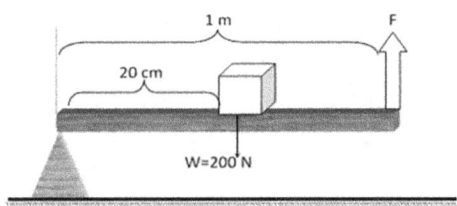

a. 1/5
b. 5
c. 1/2
d. 2

15. What is the effort-distance for the system shown?

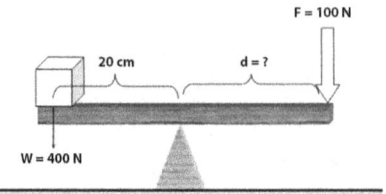

   a. 5 cm
   b. 40 cm
   c. 80 cm
   d. 100 cm

16. A door handle is an example of

   a. Inclined plane
   b. Pulley
   c. Screw
   d. Lever

17. The values of the acting force and the load are F = 20 N and P = 100 N respectively for the system shown. The total length of the lever rod is 120 cm. What is the distance between the force and the fulcrum (support) in cm?

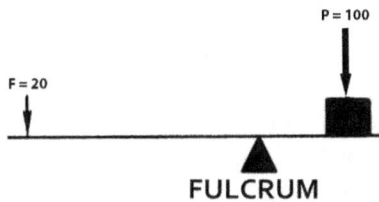

a. 70
b. 80
c. 90
d. 100

18. If the weight of the homogeneous rod is 10 N, what must be the load on the other end of the rod be to balance it?

a. 5 N
b. 10 N
c. 20 N
d. 40 N

19. **Newton's laws of motion consist of three physical laws that form the basis for classical mechanics. Which of the following is/are not included in these laws?**

    a. Unless acted upon by a force, a body at rest stays at rest.

    b. Unless acted upon by a force, a body in motion will change direction and gradually slow until it eventually stops.

    c. To every action, there is an equal and opposite reaction.

    d. A body acted upon by a force will accelerate in the same direction as the force at a magnitude that is directly proportional to the force.

20. **Which of these statements about mechanical energy is/are true?**

    a. Mechanical energy is the energy that is possessed by an object due to its motion or due to its position.

    b. Mechanical energy can be either kinetic energy (energy of motion) or potential energy (stored energy of position).

    c. Objects have mechanical energy if they are in motion

    d. All of the above.

Answer Key

Reading Comprehension

1. A
Choice B is incorrect; the author did not express their opinion on the subject matter. Choice C is incorrect, the author was not trying to prove a point, nor is the author trying to persuade.

2. C
Choice C is correct; historians believe it was brutal and bloody. Choice A is incorrect; there is no consensus that the Crusades achieved great things. Choice B is incorrect; it did not stabilize the Holy Lands. Choice D is incorrect, some historians do believe this was the purpose but not all historians.

3. D
The feudal system led to infighting. Choice A is incorrect, it had the opposite effect. Choice B is incorrect, though this is a good answer, it is not the best answer. The Church asked for volunteers not the Feudal Lords. Choice C is incorrect, it did have an effect on the Crusades.

4. A
Saracen was a generic term for Muslims widely used in Europe during the later medieval era.

5. B
This warranty does not cover a product that you have tried to fix yourself. From paragraph two, "This limited warranty does not cover ... any unauthorized disassembly, repair, or modification. "

6. C
ABC Electric could either replace or repair the fan, provided the other conditions are met. ABC Electric has the option to repair or replace.

7. B

The warranty does not cover a stove damaged in a flood. From the passage, "This limited warranty does not cover any damage to the product from improper installation, accident, abuse, misuse, natural disaster, insufficient or excessive electrical supply, abnormal mechanical or environmental conditions."

A flood is an "abnormal environmental condition," and a natural disaster, so it is not covered.

8. A

A missing part is an example of defective workmanship. This is an error made in the manufacturing process. A defective part is not considered workmanship.

9. D

This question tests the reader's summarization skills. The other choices A, B, and C focus on portions of the second paragraph that are too narrow and do not relate to the specific portion of text in question. The complexity of the sentence may mislead students into selecting one of these answers, but rearranging or restating the sentence will lead the reader to the correct answer. In addition, choice A makes an assumption that may or may not be true about the intentions of the company, choice B focuses on one product rather than the idea of the products, and choice C makes an assumption about women that may or may not be true and is not supported by the text.

10. B

This question tests reader's attention to detail. If a reader selects A, he or she may have picked up on the use of the word "debate" and assumed, very logically, that the two are at odds because they are fighting; however, this is simply not supported in the text. Choice C also uses very specific quotes from the text, but it rearranges and gives them false meaning. The artists want to elevate their creations above the creations of other artists, thereby showing that they are "creative" and "innovative." Similarly, choice D takes phrases straight from the text and rearranges and confuses them. The artists are described as wanting to be "creative, innovative, individual people," not the women.

11. A

This question tests reader's vocabulary and summarization skills. This phrase, used by the author, may seem flippant and dismissive if readers focus on the word "whatever" and misinterpret it as a popular, colloquial term. In this way, Choices B and C may mislead the reader to selecting one of them by including the terms "unimportant" and "stupid," respectively. Choice D is a similar misreading, but doesn't make sense when the phrase is at the beginning of the passage and the entire passage is on media messages. Choice A is literally and contextually appropriate, and the reader can understand that the author would like to keep the introduction focused on the topic the passage is going to discuss.

12. A

This question tests a reader's inference skills. The extreme use of the word "all" in choice B suggests that every single advertising company are working to be approachable, and while this is not only unlikely, the text specifically states that "more" companies have done this, signifying that they have not all participated, even if it's a possibility that they may some day. The use of the limiting word "only" in choice C lends that answer similar problems; women are still buying from companies who do not care about this message, or those companies would not be in business, and the passage specifies that "many" women are worried about media messages, but not all. Readers may find choice D logical, especially if they are looking to make an inference, and while this may be a possibility, the passage does not suggest or discuss this happening. Choice A is correct based on specifically because of the relation between "still working" in the answer and "will hopefully" and the extensive discussion on companies struggles, which come only with progress, in the text.

13. C

This question tests the reader's summarization skills. The entire passage is leading up to the idea that the president of the US may not have had grounds to assert his Fourteen Points when other countries had lost so much. Choice A is pretty directly inferred by the text, but it does not adequately summarize what the entire passage is trying to communicate. Choice B may also be inferred by the passage when it says that the war is "imminent," but it does not represent the entire message, either. The passage does seem to be in praise of FDR, or at least in respect of him, but it does not in any way claim that he is the smartest president, nor does this represent the many other points included. Choice C is then the obvious answer, and most directly relates to the closing sentences which it rewords.

14. C
This question tests the reader's attention to detail. The passage does state that choices A and B are true, and while those statements are in proximity to the explanation for why the war started, they are not the reason given. Choice D is a mix up of words used in the passage, which says that the largest powers were in play but not that this fact somehow started the war. The passage does make a direct statement that a domino effect started the war, supporting choice C as the correct answer.

15. A
This question tests the reader's understanding of functions in writing. Throughout the passage, it states that leaders of other nations were hesitant to accept generous or peaceful terms because of the grievances of the war, and the great loss of life was chief among these. While the passage does touch on the devastation of deadly weapons (B), the use of this raw, emotional fact serves a larger purpose, and the focus of the passage is not weapons. While readers may indeed consider who lost the most soldiers (C) when, so many countries were involved and the inequalities of loss are mentioned in the passage, there is no discussion of this in the passage. Choice D is related to A, but choice A is more direct and relates more to the passage.

16. B
This question tests the reader's vocabulary skills. Choice A may seem appealing to readers because it is phonetically similar to "catalyzed," but the two are not related in any other way. Choice C makes sense in context, but if plugged in to the sentence creates a redundancy that doesn't make sense. Choice D does also not make sense contextually, even if the reader may consider that funds were needed to create more weaponry, especially if it was advanced.

17. A
The correct order of ingredients is brown sugar, baking soda and chocolate chips.

18. B
Sturdy: strong, solid in structure or person. In context, Stir in chocolate chips by hand with a *sturdy* wooden spoon.

19. A
Disperse: to scatter in different directions or break up. In context, Stir until the chocolate chips and nuts are evenly *dispersed*.

20. B
You can stop stirring the nuts when they are evenly distributed. From the passage, "Stir until the chocolate chips and nuts are evenly dispersed."

21. B
The time limit for radar detectors is 14 days. Since you made the purchase 15 days ago, you do not qualify for the guarantee.

22. B
Since you made the purchase 10 days ago, you are covered by the guarantee. Since it is an advertised price at a different store, ABC Electric will "beat" the price by 10% of the difference, which is,

500 – 400 = 100 – difference in price

100 X 10% = $10 – 10% of the difference

The advertised lower price is $400. ABC will beat this price by 10% so they will refund $100 + 10 = $110.

23. C
The purpose of this passage is to persuade.

24. B
The correct answer can be found in the fourth sentence of the first paragraph.

Choice A is incorrect because repenting begins the day AFTER Mardi Gras. Choice C is incorrect because you can celebrate Mardi Gras without being a member of a Krewe.

Choice D is incorrect because exploration does not play any role in a modern Mardi Gras celebration.

25. A
The second sentence is the last paragraph states that Krewes are led by the Kings and Queens. Therefore, you must have to be part of a Krewe to be its King or its Queen.

Choice B is incorrect because it never states in the passage that only people from France can be Kings and Queen of Mardi Gras

Choice C is incorrect because the passage says nothing about having to speak French.

Choice D is incorrect because the passage does state that the Kings and Queens throw doubloons, which is fake money.

26. C
The first sentences of BOTH the 2nd and 3rd paragraphs mention that French explorers started this tradition in New Orleans.
Choices A, B and D are incorrect because they are names of cities or countries listed in the 2nd paragraph.

27. B
In the final paragraph, the word spectator is used to describe people who are watching the parade and catching cups, beads and doubloons.

Choices A and C are incorrect because we know the people who participate are part of Krewes. People who work the floats and parades are also part of Krewes

Choice D is incorrect because the passage makes no mention of people who do not celebrate Mardi Gras.

28. A
Caterpillars spend most of their time eating.

PRACTICE TEST QUESTIONS 2

29. B
Some caterpillars are herbivores, others eat other insects (carnivores).

30. B
From the passage, the ants provide some degree of protection.

MATHEMATICS

1. A
2 + a number divided by 7.
(2 + X) divided by 7.
(2 + X)/7

2. B
Total Volume = Volume of large cylinder - Volume of small cylinder

Volume of a cylinder = area of base * height = $\pi r^2 * h$

Total Volume = ($\pi * 12^2 * 10$) - ($\pi * 6^2 * 5$) = $1440\pi - 180\pi$

= 1260π in^3

3. C
1 hour is equal to 3,600 seconds and 1 kilometer is equal to 1000 meters.

Since this train travels 72 kilometers per hour, this means that it covers 72,000 meters in 3,600 seconds.

If it travels 72,000 meters in 3,600 seconds

It travels x meters in 12 seconds

By cross multiplication: x = 72,000 * 12 / 3,600

x = 240 meters

4. A
Let us first mention the money Tony spent: $80

Now we need to find the money Tony earned:

He had 15 dozen eggs = 15 * 12 = 180 eggs. 16 eggs were broken. So,

Remaining number of eggs that Tony sold = 180 − 16 = 164.

Total amount he earned for selling 164 eggs = 164 * 0.54 = $88.56.

As a summary, he spent $80 and earned $88.56.

The profit is the difference: 88.56 - 80 = $8.56

Percentage profit is found by proportioning the profit to the money he spent:

8.56 * 100/80 = 10.7%

Checking the answers, we round 10.7 to the nearest whole number: 11%

5. A
If we know the coordinates of two points on a line, we can find the slope (m) with the below formula:

$m = (y_2 - y_1)/(x_2 - x_1)$ where (x_1, y_1) represent the coordinates of one point and (x_2, y_2) the other.

In this question:

$(-9, 6)$: $x_1 = -9$, $y_1 = 6$

$(18, -18)$: $x_2 = 18$, $y_2 = -18$

Inserting these values into the formula:

m = (-18 - 6)/(18 - (-9)) = (-24)/(27) ... Simplifying by 3:

m = -8/9

6. B
Number of absent students = 83 − 72 = 11

Percentage of absent students is found by proportioning the number of absent students to total number of students in the class = (11 * 100)/83 = 13.25

Checking the answers, we round 13.25 to the nearest whole number: 13%

7. B
$ab^2 (9+8) = 17ab^2$

8. B
Total expense is $2000 and we are informed that $5 is spent per meter. Combining these two information, we know that the total length of the fence is 2000/5 = 400 meters.

The fence is built around a square-shaped field. If one side of the square is "a," the perimeter of the square is "4a." Here, the perimeter is equal to 400 meters. So,

400 = 4a

100 = a → this means that one side of the square is equal to 100 meters

9. A
If we know the coordinates of two points on a line, we can find the slope (m) with the below formula:
$m = (y_2 - y_1)/(x_2 - x_1)$ where (x_1, y_1) represent the coordinates of one point and (x_2, y_2) the other.

In this question:

$(-4, y_1) : x_1 = -4, y_1 =$ we will find

$(-8, 7) : x_2 = -8, y_2 = 7$

$m = -7/4$

Inserting these values into the formula:

$-7/4 = (7 - y_1)/(-8 - (-4))$

$-7/4 = (7 - y_1)/(-8 + 4)$

$7/(-4) = (7 - y_1)/(-4)$ ... Simplifying the denominators of both sides by -4:

$7 = 7 - y_1$

$0 = -y_1$

$y_1 = 0$

10. D
To find the total turnout in all three polling stations, we need to proportion the number of voters to the number of all registered voters.
Total number of voters = 945 + 860 + 1210 = 3015

Total number of registered voters = 1270 + 1050 + 1440 = 3760

Percentage turnout in all three polling stations = 3015 * 100/3760 = 80.19%

Check the answer, round 80.19 to the nearest whole number: 80%

11. D
Area of Type B consists of two rectangles and a half circle. We can find these three areas and sum them up to find the total area:

Area of the left rectangle: (4 + 8) * 8 = 96 m²

Area of the right rectangle: 14 * 8 = 112 m²

The diameter of the circle is equal to 14 m. So, the radius is 14/2 = 7:

Area of the half circle = $(1/2) * \pi r^2$ = (1/2) * (22/7) * (7)² = (1 * 22 * 49)/(2 * 7) = 77 m²

Area of Type B = 96 + 112 + 77 = 285 m²

Converting this area to ft²: 285 m² = 285 * 10.76 ft² = 3066.6 ft²

Type B is (3066.6 - 1300 = 1766.6 ft²) 1766.6 ft² larger than type A.

12. B
Based on this graph, a person that is 85 will make 31.3 visits to the hospital every year.

13. A
Based on this graph, the number of visits per year is going up as age goes up, so we can expect a person that is 95 to have more than 31.3 visits to the hospital each year.

14. A

The formula of the volume of cylinder is the base area multiplied by the height. As the formula:

Volume of a cylinder = πr²h. Where π is 3.142, r is radius of the cross sectional area, and h is the height.

We know that the diameter is 5 meters, so the radius is 5/2 = 2.5 meters.

The volume is: V = 3.142 * 2.5² * 12 = 235.65 m³.

15. C

The large cube is made up of 8 smaller cubes with 5 cm sides. The volume of a cube is found by the third power of the length of one side.

Volume of the large cube = Volume of the small cube * 8

= (5³) * 8 = 125 * 8

= 1000 cm³

There is another solution for this question. Find the side length of the large cube. There are two cubes rows with 5 cm length for each. So, one side of the large cube is 10 cm.

The volume of this large cube is equal to 10³ = 1000 cm³

16. B
1 US gallon = 3.78541178 liters

17. C
Pythagorean Theorem:
(Hypotenuse)² = (Perpendicular)² + (Base)²
h² = a² + b²

Given: a = 6, h = 10
h² = a² + b²
b² = h² - a²
b² = 10² + 6²
b² = 100 − 36
b² = 64
b = 8

18. A
60/x = 75/100
60* 100/X = 75
6000/75 = X
X = 80

19. D
Two parallel lines intersected by a third line with angles of 75°
x = 75° (corresponding angles)
x + y = 180° (supplementary angles)
y = 180° - 75°
y = 105°

20. C
71 ÷ 1000 = 0.071.

21. A
.33 × .59 = .1947

22. D
Two parallel lines (m & side AB) intersected by side AC. This means that 50° and a angles are interior angles. So:
a = 50° (interior angles).

23. A
Collect like terms, 7x = 47 + 9 = 56,
divide both sides by 7
x = 8

24. C
The ten thousandths place in 1.7389 will be the 4th decimal place, 9.

25. A
.87 - .48 = 0.39.

26. C
Forty nine thousandths will place the '9' in the 3rd decimal place, 0.049.

27. C
a. 3/4 * 2/2 = 6/8
b. 3/4 * 3/3 = 9/12
c. 3/4 * 4/4 = 12/18 – Incorrect!

28. A
   a. 84/231 = 12/33 > 1/3
   b. 6/35 = 1/5 < 1/3
   c. 3/22 = 1/7 < 1/3

29. C
Here are the choices:
a. 1
b. $\sqrt{2}$ = 1.414
c. 3/2 = 1.5   Largest number
d. 4/3 = 1.33

30. B
Collecting similar terms (algebraic addition).
2b + 9b – 5b = 11b - 5b = 6b

31. D
Remove parenthesis
$4Y^3 - 2Y^2 + 7Y^2 + 3Y - Y$
add and subtract like terms, $4Y^3 + 5Y^2 + 2Y$

32. C
4.7 + .9 + .01 = 5.61.

33. D
Open parenthesis, (7 x 2y + 7 x 8) + 1- (4 x y -20) =
14y + 56 + 1 - 4y - 20,
Collect like terms =14y -4y + 56 + 1 – 20 = 10y + 37

34. D
The distance between two points is found by
$= [(x_2 - x_1)^2 + (y_2 - y_1)^2]^{1/2}$

In this question:

(18, 12) : x_1 = 18, y_1 = 12

(9, -6) : x_2 = 9, y_2 = -6

Distance = $[(9 - 18)^2 + (-6 - 12)^2]^{1/2}$

$= [(-9)^2 + (-18)^2]^{1/2}$

$= (9^2 + 2^2 * 9^2)^{1/2}$

$= (9^2(1 + 5))^{1/2}$ ... We can take 9 out of the square root:

$= 9 * 6^{1/2}$

$= 9\sqrt{6}$

$= 9 * 2.45$

$= 22.04$

The distance is approximately 22 units.

35. D
60% of x = 12

$(60/100)x = 12$

$60x = 1200$

$x = 20$

36. D
$.84/.7 = 1.2$

37. C
$6x - 24 = 3x + 12$
$6x - 3x = 12 + 24$
$3x = 36$
$x = 12$

38. D
We have a circle given with diameter 8 cm and a square located within the circle. We are asked to find the area of the circle for which we only need to know the length of the radius that is the half of the diameter.
Area of circle = πr^2 ... r = 8/2 = 4 cm

Area of circle = $\pi * 4^2$

= 16π cm² ... As we notice, the inner square has no role in this question.

39. B
Perimeter of a parallelogram is the sum of the sides.
Perimeter = 2(l + b)
Perimeter = 2(3 +10), 2 x 13
Perimeter = 26 cm.

40. D
He pays 'ns' amount to the employees for 7 days. The 'x' amount will be for '7x/ns' days.

41. C
Converting a percentage to a decimal – divide the numerator by the denominator.
87 ÷ 100 = 0.87.

42. C
Volume of a cylinder is $\pi \times r^2 \times h$
Diameter = 5 ft. so radius is 2.5 ft.
Volume of cylinder= $\pi \times 2.5^2 \times 2$
= $\pi \times 6.25 \times 2 = 12.5 \pi$
Approximate π to 3.142
Volume of the cylinder = 39.25

Volume of a rectangle = height X width X length.
= 5 X 5 X 4 = 100

Total volume = Volume of rectangular solid + volume of cylinder
Total volume = 100 + 39.25
Total volume = 139.25 ft^3 or about 140 ft^3

43. D
The jacket costs $545.00 so we can round up to $550. 10% of $550 is 55. We can round down to $50, which is easier to work with. $550 - $50 is $500. The jacket will cost about $500.

The actual cost will be 10% X 545 = $54.50
545 – 54.50 = $490.50

44. A
Five greater than 3 times a number.
5 + 3 times a number.
5 + 3X

45. B
If we know the coordinates of two points on a line, we can find the slope (m) with the below formula:
$m = (y_2 - y_1)/(x_2 - x_1)$ where (x_1, y_1) represent the coordinates of one point and (x_2, y_2) the other.

In this question:

$(-4, -4) : x_1 = -4, y_1 = -4$

$(-1, 2) : x_2 = -1, y_2 = 2$

Inserting these values into the formula:

$m = (2 - (-4))/(-1 - (-4)) = (2 + 4)/(-1 + 4) = 6/3$ ... Simplifying by 3:

m = 2

46. C
Pythagorean Theorem:
$(Hypotenuse)^2 = (Perpendicular)^2 + (Base)^2$
$h^2 = a^2 + b^2$

Given: $3^2 + 4^2 = h^2$
$h^2 = 9 + 16$
$h = \sqrt{25}$
h = 5

47. D
First calculate total square feet, which is 15 X 24 = 360 sq. ft. Next convert to square yards, (1 sq. ft. = 0.1111 sq. yards) which is 360 X 0.1111 = 39.9999 or 40 square yards. At $0.50 per square yard, the total cost is $20.

48. B
Flat Screen TVs are the third best-selling product.

49. B
The two products that are closest in the number of sales, are Flat Screen TVs and Radar Detectors.

50. C
Comparing respective sides, ABCD, KLMN, WXYZ are similar.

MECHANICAL COMPREHENSION

1. C

The block and tackle system composed of a system of pulleys as shown operates according the following rule:

Pulling Force = Load / (Number of supporting ropes)

Here Load and Weight are the same thing.

Here, the number of supporting ropes is 4. So, we have

F = 360/4

Force = 90 N Choice C

Feedback for Choice D

Do not confuse the number of supporting ropes. The rope which is being pulled is not counted. Otherwise, you will obtain the wrong answer choice D 72 (360 / 5).

2. A
The equation of meshed gears states that the speed of rotation V (in rot/s) is inversely proportional to the number of teeth N. Mathematically,
VA/VB = NB/NA

From the figure, it is obvious that NA = 20 and NB = 35. So, since the time of rotation for both gears is equal, we have

VA/100 = 35/20

VB = (100 × 35)/20 = 175 turns

3. C

Choice A is correct. Gears are teethed wheels used to generate rotation.

Choice B is correct. Meshed gears move at the same time as they are connected.

Choice C is false. Meshed gears move at different speed depending on their size. Larger gears move slower than smaller gears.

Choice D is correct. Teeth in gears help increase the friction and avoid slipping.

4. A

If the pinion rotates clockwise, its lower teeth move due left. Therefore, the rack shifts left as well.

5. B

If the rack shifts to the right, the lower part of the pinion moves right as well. This means the entire pinion rotates counter-clockwise.

6. A

The equation of levers is
Load × Load distance = Force × Force distance

Here, the load is represented by the symbol P (force is F). On the other hand, Load distance is 2 units and force distance = 3 units.

The mechanical advantage of levers is
MA = Load/Force = (Force distance)/(Load distance)

7. D

The ratio of the load to the effort is known as Mechanical Advantage (MA). It shows how many times easier it would be to perform an action using the simple machine compared to not using it. Mechanical advantage has no unit.

8. A

A lateral view of the Wheel and Axle system is shown on the right. The pivot is at the common center of the two circles. Force is on the left side and Load is on the right one. Therefore, this is an example of first class lever (Force – Pivot –

Load).

9. C
Sugar tongs have their turning point at one side and the load is on the other side. We must use a force between them to catch the sugar cubes. Therefore, this is an example of third class levers (Pivot – Force – Load).

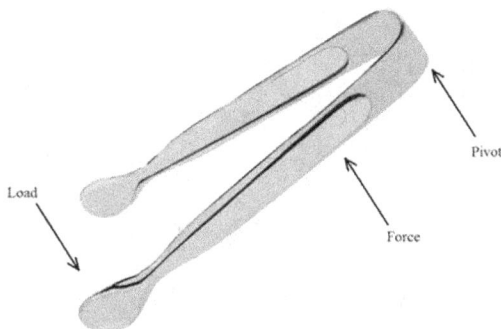

10. D
This is a combined system of simple machines composed of a Wheel and Axle and a Movable pulley system.

For the wheel and axle, the mechanical advantage is $MA_1 = R / r$. Here, $MA1 = 3$.

For movable pulleys, the mechanical advantage MA_2 is 2. So, the combined mechanical advantage is
$MA_{total} = MA_1 \times MA_2 = 3 \times 2 = 6$.

This means the force needed to lift the load is 6 time smaller than the load itself. So, $F/W = 1/6$

11. B
Since the system is in equilibrium, we have the total clockwise moment (turning effect) is equal to the counter clockwise one. The equation used in this situation is
$F_1 * d_1 = F_2 * d_2 + F_3 * d_3$

Or
$m_1 * g * d_1 = m_2 * g * d_2 + m_3 * g * d_3$
Simplifying gravity g from both sides and giving that $d_1 = 3$ units, $d_2 = 1$ unit and $d_3 = 4$ units, the equation becomes,

$4 * 3 = 2 * 1 + m_3 * 4$
$12 = 2 + m_3 * 4$
$m_3 * 4 = 12 - 2 = 10$
$m_3 = 10/4 = 2.5$ kg

12. C

First, we must find the weight of the hanging object on the left.

$W_{left} * d_{left} = W_{right} * d_{right}$
$W_{left} * 4$ units $= 40N * 2$ units
$W_{left} = (40N * 2$ units$) / (4$ units$) = 20N$

The total weight supported by the bar is 40N + 10N = 60N.

This value also corresponds to the reading of the dynamo-meter.

13. D

The bar weight tries to rotate the system clockwise. The weight is exerted at middle of the bar (d_w = 3 units). This is balanced by the pulling force of the rope exerted at 4 units away from the turning point (support). Thus, the upward force exerted by the rope is calculated by

$W_{bar} d_w = F_{rope} * d_F$

From the figure, you can see that the rope is connected to a combined pulley system (one fixed and one movable). Thus, given that only the movable pulley provides a gain in force (precisely double), we have for $F_{rope} = 2 * 3N = 6N$. So, we can write

$W_{bar} * 3$ units $= 6N * 4$ units
$W_{bar} = (6N * 4$ units$) / (3$ units$) = 8N$

14. B

The mechanical advantage of a lever (second class in the specific case) is calculated in two ways:

MA = W/F or MA = d_F/dW

The second equation is more suitable here, as we have enough information. So,

MA = 1m/20cm = 1m/0.2m = 5

15. C
The effort is represented here through the letter F (force). Thus, given that in pivoting systems in equilibrium

$W \cdot d_w = F \cdot d_F$

The equation becomes, after the substitutions,

400 N · 20cm = 100N · d_F
d_F = (400 N · 20cm) / 100N
= 80cm

16. D
The door handle has a turning effect when a force acts on it. Therefore, it is an example of a Lever (first class) as the turning point is between the force and load (they are on opposite sides of the door).

17. D
To create equilibrium, we must have:

$P \cdot d_P = F \cdot d_F$

If the required force distance d_F is denoted by x, the load distance d_P is 120 − x. Thus, we can write

100 · (120 - x) = 20 · x

Simplifying both sides by 20, the equation becomes,

5 · (120 - x) = x

5 · 120 − 5 · x = x

5 · 120 = x + 5x

600 = 6x

X = 600/6 = 100cm

18. A
If we use a force in the right side of the bar, the equation becomes, an example of a first class lever in which pivot is located between Load and Force.

The equation of levers is

Load × Load distance = Force × Force distance

Here, Load = 10N, Force is unknown,
Load distance = 2 units, and Force distance = 4 units.
Thus,

10N × 2units = F × 4units
F = (10N × 2 units) / 4units
F = 5N

19. B
Unless acted upon by a force, a body in motion will change direction and gradually slow until it eventually stops.

This answer is related to Newton's 1st law of motion which states that: Unless acted upon by a force, a body at rest stays at rest, and a moving body continues moving at the same speed in a straight line

20. A
All of the statements are true.

Supplemental Practice

https://courses.test-preparation.ca/course/ironworker-supplemental

Over 350 extra questions

Use Coupon - IronWorker

CONCLUSION

CONGRATULATIONS! You have made it this far because you have applied yourself diligently to practicing for the exam and no doubt improved your potential score considerably! Getting into a good school is a huge step in a journey that might be challenging at times but will be many times more rewarding and fulfilling. That is why being prepared is so important.

Study then Practice and then Succeed!

Good Luck!

https://www.facebook.com/CompleteTestPreparation/

https://www.youtube.com/user/MrTestPreparation

ONLINE RESOURCES

How to Prepare for a Test - The Ultimate Guide

https://www.test-preparation.ca/the-ultimate-guide-to-test-preparation-strategy/

Learning Styles - The Complete Guide

https://www.test-preparation.ca/learning-styles/

Test Anxiety Secrets!

https://www.test-preparation.ca/how-to-overcome-test-anxiety/

Time Management on a Test

https://www.test-preparation.ca/test-tactics-the-time-wise-approach/

Flash Cards - The Complete Guide

https://www.test-preparation.ca/test-preparation-with-flash-cards/

Test Preparation Video Series

https://www.test-preparation.ca/video-series-on-test-preparation-multiple-choice-strategies-and-how-to-study/

How to Memorize - The Complete Guide

https://www.test-preparation.ca/a-guide-to-memorizing-anything-easily-and-painlessly/